The Journey begins...

Path to Certainty
: a BIG BIM Chronology

> FRANK LLOYD WRIGHT SAID, "MAN BUILT MOST NOBLY WHEN LIMITATIONS WERE AT THEIR GREATEST."

Finith E. Jernigan, AIA

Living better, saving money, and staying profitable is what BIM is all about.

Do better work, more efficiently—become more successful.

Over the last century, architects began to concentrate on the design phase, with minimal overlap into other areas. This focus created a very cyclic business process. Working in what is now an antiquated business process, architects have been losing their leadership role. Owners demand improved management of projects.

There are proven techniques to correct the problem. Dr. Eliyahu Goldratt theorized that any business could improve its bottom line results through applying scientific methods to resolving organizational problems. Each business has a single constraint that limits its performance relative to its goal. That is what BIM is about.

4Site Press

130 East Main Street
Salisbury, MD 21801-5038, USA
fulfillment@4sitesystems.com
http://www.4sitesystems.com

Jernigan, Finith E.
Path to Certainty : a BIM Chronology / [Finith E. Jernigan]. -- 1st ed.p. cm.

ISBN-13: 978-0-9795699-3-7
ISBN-10: 0-9795699-3-1

Publisher: 4Site Press, Salisbury, Maryland
Printed in the United States

1970s History

EXTRA EXTRA...

BURY THE OLD WAYS *WITH BIG BIM*

> ALVIN TOFFLER POPULARIZED THE CONCEPTS OF "MASS CUSTOMIZATION" AND "JUST-IN-TIME PRODUCTION." YOU CAN USE THE CONCEPTS TO MAKE INTEGRATION HAPPEN.

The solution began to take form in the 1970s.

The '70s were an era of confusion, conflict, and change. McGovern lost to Nixon in 1972, and by 1974, Nixon had resigned. Intergraph was getting off the ground and AutoCAD was not on the horizon. The anti-war movement was in full swing. The floppy disk and the microprocessor had recently appeared, but most of us were still punching cards—if we used computers at all. Most considered Toyota to be a cheap import aimed at those with limited resources. Ford Motors was the gold standard. Futurism was in full swing. The possibilities were endless.

- Impact things far into the future

- Increase the chance of future success

- Manage by constraints

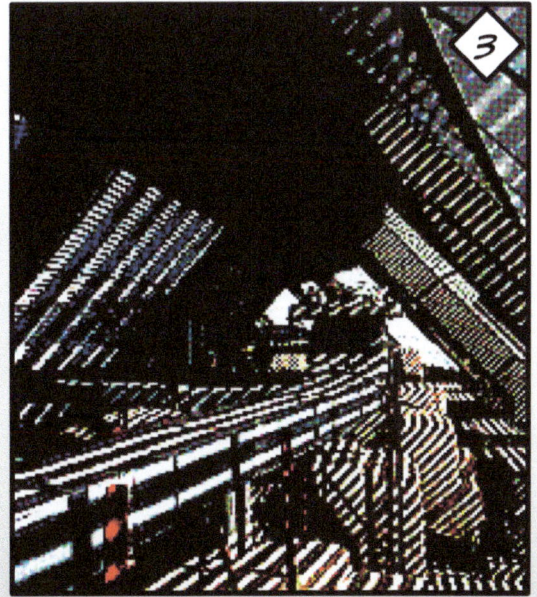

By the mid-1980s, there was more and hungrier competitors.

Economic conditions changed. Staff expected higher salaries and clients demanded more in less time. Computers were becoming an issue. Construction management and design/build proved that it is more cost effective to have all of the issues examined as early in the process as possible. Projects that were properly budgeted and designed within the budget had a much higher chance of success.

THE EASY CHOICES ARE THE ONES YOU MAKE WHEN YOU DON'T KNOW ENOUGH TO SEE HOW COMPLICATED THINGS ARE...

Saudi Arabia

In the late-1980s we looked at everything on the market—worldwide.

We concentrated on products that would work within an agency construction management approach and developed a rough business case for the process.

Egypt

Turkey

Firenze

USING MODELS TO PROTOTYPE SOLUTIONS IS NOT A NEW CONCEPT!

1980s

AUGUST 1983

FINITH BEGINS THE QUEST *FOR BIG BIM IN TURKEY*

ALVIN TOFFLER, WROTE THAT "THE CAPTURE OF INTEGRATED KNOWLEDGE IN AN ORGANIZED WAY SHOULD DRIVE PLANNING. ATTEMPTS TO BRING THIS KNOWLEDGE TOGETHER WOULD CONSTITUTE ONE OF THE CROWNING INTELLECTUAL EFFORTS IN HISTORY—AND ONE OF THE MOST WORTHWHILE."

Politics

1990s

> FOR MANY OWNERS, THE BENEFITS FROM VIRTUAL DESIGN ARE POLITICAL. THESE NEW PROCESSES GIVE DEPENDABLE INFORMATION, EARLY IN THE PROCESS, HEADING OFF PROBLEMS AND HEADACHES.

What's in it for ME?

- Don't forget how and how much

- Invest up front for downstream benefits

- Focus attention and talent on the earliest steps in the process

Studies suggest that owners experience schedule and cost overruns on 85% of all projects.

From the day that virtual design tools arrived, they made life easier. Better visualization, more coordinated documents and improved client communication are, by themselves, enough reason to use BIM for every project.

> CONVERSIONS AND ADAPTIVE REUSE PROJECTS ARE IDEAL CANDIDATES FOR VIRTUAL DESIGN.

Virtual Design enables the change...

- Just in time decisions & better information

- Minimizes rework

- True collaboration & sharing

- Better work...of greater value

PUBLIC SCHOOL PROJECTS USED BIM PROCESSES FROM THE MID-1990'S.

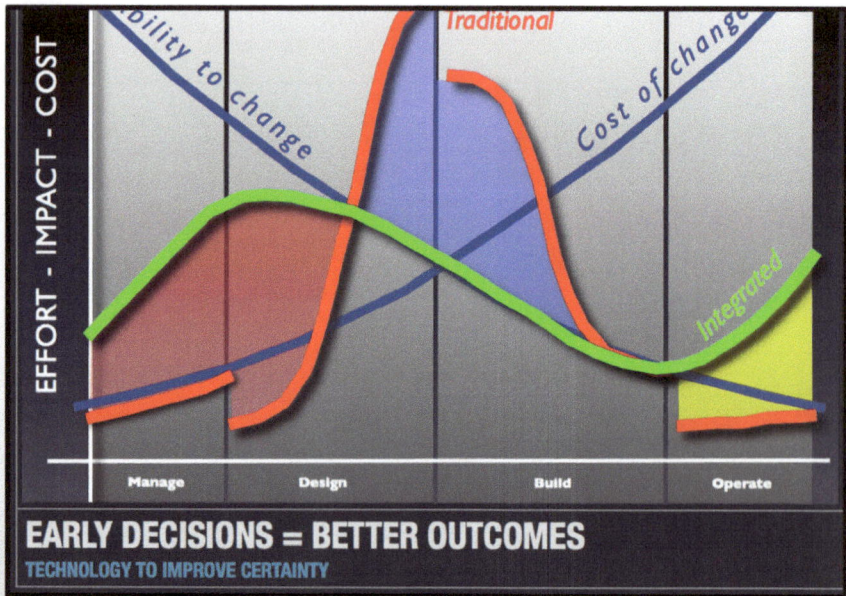

EFFORT - IMPACT - COST

Ability to change

Traditional

Cost of change

Integrated

Manage | Design | Build | Operate

EARLY DECISIONS = BETTER OUTCOMES
TECHNOLOGY TO IMPROVE CERTAINTY

IN THE EARLY 1990S, WE FOUND THE TECHNOLOGY THAT WOULD SOLVE THE PROBLEM AND BEGAN TO LOOK AT HOW WE COULD TWEAK OUR PROCESS TO MAKE IT HAPPEN.

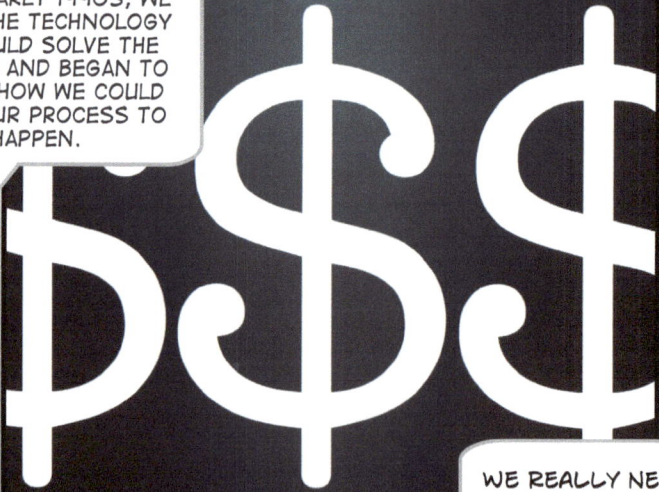

Virtual design is about doing the best design and construction in the most economical and sustainable way. With a minimum of missteps, errors and problems.

WE REALLY NEED TO AGREE ON A NAME FOR THIS... WE NEED AN EASY WAY FOR OTHERS TO UNDERSTAND WHAT YOU ARE TALKING ABOUT!

MARCH 1992

ArchiCAD
ARCHICAD 4.0 REFERENCE MAN

FINITH FINDS THE TOOLS
FOR BIG BIM

Use tools and processes that work well—right now. Take advantage of new technologies as they become commercially available.

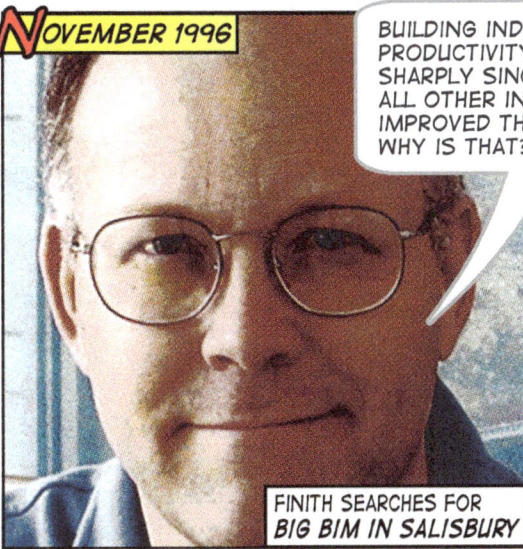

FINITH SEARCHES FOR
BIG BIM IN SALISBURY

BUILDING INDUSTRY PRODUCTIVITY HAS DECLINED SHARPLY SINCE COMPUTERS. ALL OTHER INDUSTRIES HAVE IMPROVED THEIR PRODUCTIVITY. WHY IS THAT?

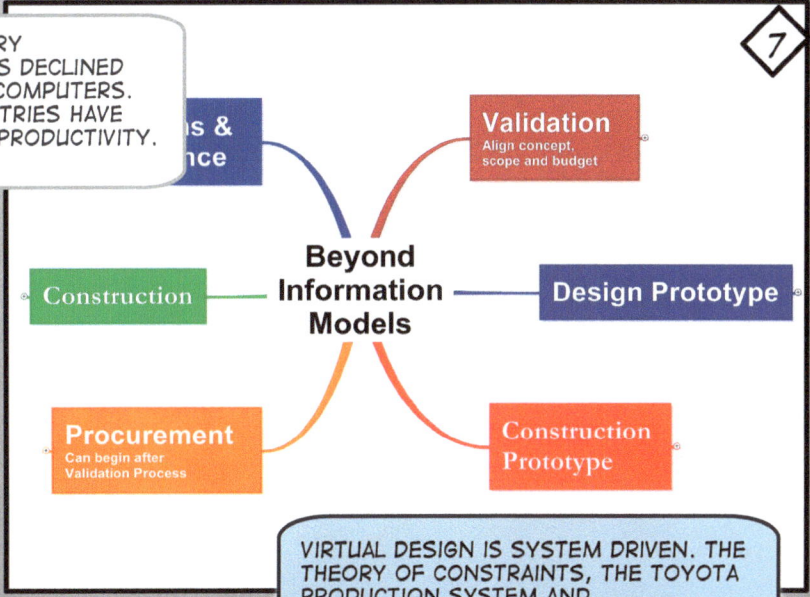

Beyond Information Models

- ...s & ...nce
- **Validation** — Align concept, scope and budget
- **Construction**
- **Design Prototype**
- **Procurement** — Can begin after Validation Process
- **Construction Prototype**

VIRTUAL DESIGN IS SYSTEM DRIVEN. THE THEORY OF CONSTRAINTS, THE TOYOTA PRODUCTION SYSTEM AND CONSTRUCTION MANAGEMENT ALL DEFINE THE PATH. UNDERSTAND THE UNDERLYING THEORIES AND TAILOR YOUR BUSINESS TO DELIVER THE BENEFITS.

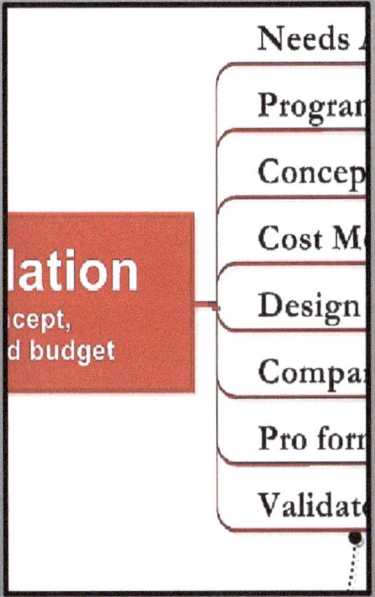

...lation — ...cept, ...d budget

- Needs ...
- Progra...
- Concep...
- Cost M...
- Design...
- Compa...
- Pro for...
- Validat...

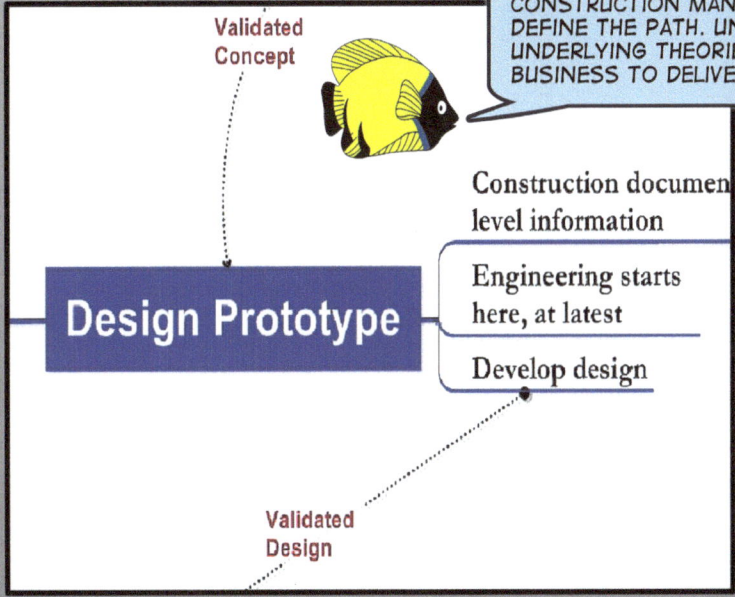

Design Prototype

Validated Concept

- Construction documen... level information
- Engineering starts here, at latest
- Develop design

Validated Design

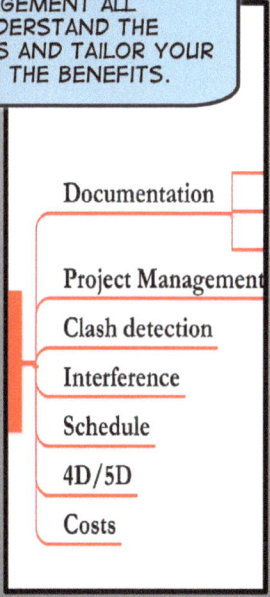

- Documentation
- Project Management
- Clash detection
- Interference
- Schedule
- 4D/5D
- Costs

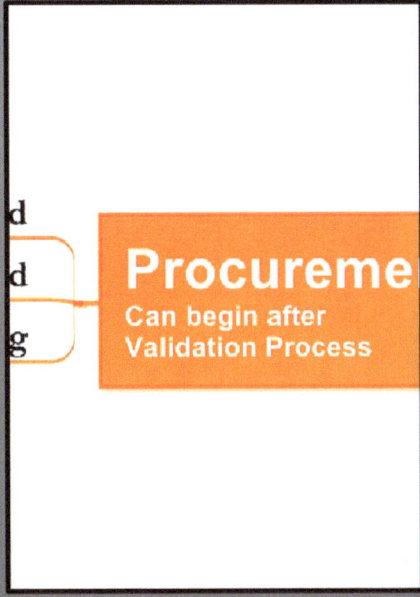

Procureme... — Can begin after Validation Process

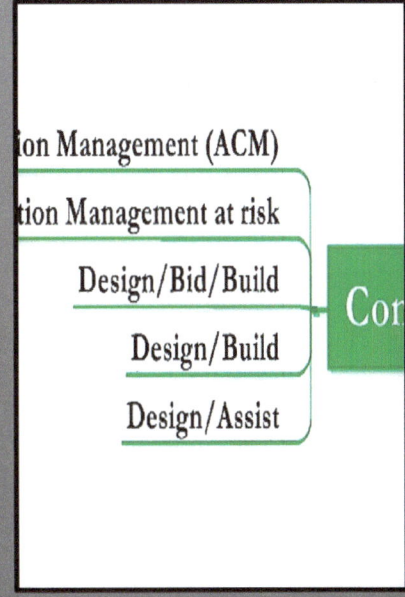

- ...ion Management (ACM)
- ...ion Management at risk
- Design/Bid/Build
- Design/Build
- Design/Assist

Con...

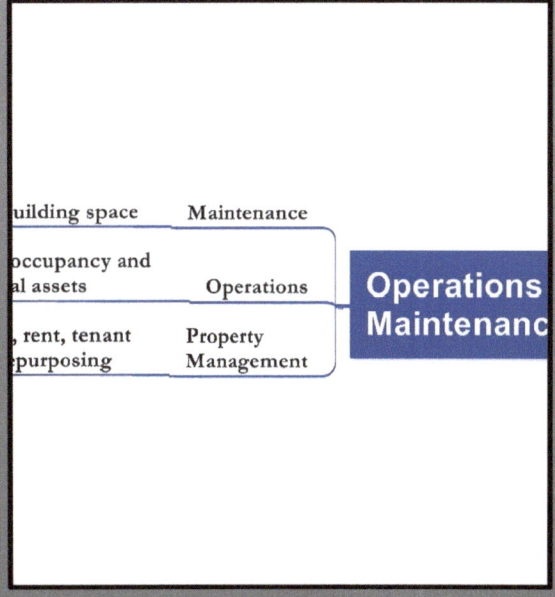

- ...uilding space
- ...occupancy and ...al assets
- ..., rent, tenant ...epurposing
- Maintenance
- Operations
- Property Management

Operations Maintenanc...

MAY 1998

FINITH STARTS TO CREATE
LIFECYCLE MODELS

Validated Concept

A squishy fish tale

Are you asking yourself—"What do squishy fish have to do with integration?" Squishy fish have everything to do with it.

Near the end of 1997, Joel Hirsh, of Hirsh -Associates mailed stress airplane tagged with "Celebrating 20 Years of Hard Analysis for a Squishy Industry." It was a cute and different way to send a holiday greeting. The cards that that year went in the trash; the squishy airplane is still on the shelf. It made a lasting impression.

The next September, we had our annual discussion about holiday mailings, looking for ways to differentiate ourselves. Frank Brady, one of our 4Site Managers, suggested that we do "something like that—pointing at Joel's airplane." Leisl Ashby, a young architect, pulled out a stress fish that she had received from a wall-covering supplier—"Why not do fish? Why not play on the ATLANTIC theme? We could even do different fish every year." The Design Atlantic Ltd squishy fish was born.

The fish became a mnemonic, a memory aid, to help communicate our corporate creed "—Reduce stress with early, dependable knowledge." The fish tie us to our roots— the Delmarva Peninsula, situated right between the Atlantic Ocean and the Chesapeake Bay. They are collectable. Clients build their collection of squishy fish over time—as we strive to do for their facilities.

In early December 1998, we sent out our first squishy fish. Every year we send out new colors of fish. Last holiday season, we sent out our tenth anniversary fish. Our friends collect them. Our clients and friends identify us with our colorful fish. Recently a longtime client, quipped—"You better send me another fish"—when he heard what his new project would cost.

Squishy fish are integrated! At interviews they help get jobs. At trade shows they get leads. We use them as stuffing in proposals. We hand them out anywhere we go. Clients call us for extra fish if we send only one. They are good conversation pieces. They are memorable.

A couple of years ago, we were hired to help a volunteer fire company develop a strategic plan. As part of the planning process, they decided to hold a three-day retreat.

Volunteer firefighters can be very passionate they are about their fire companies. When they are saving you from the burning house, their passion is a great and wonderful thing. When they are participating in a planning process, their passion can take some serious management.

The first day things got tense—and the squishy fish suddenly took on a role that we had never envisioned. The group began to use the fish to take out their frustrations, by throwing fish instead of fists. The fish provided a non-damaging outlet for the group to begin to reach a consensus.

By the end of the third day, the group created a strategic plan they could all buy into and support. We think that the fish helped.

FAIL FAST...

and

move on

- **Critical leadership skills**

  Knowing and using your resources

  Understanding the group

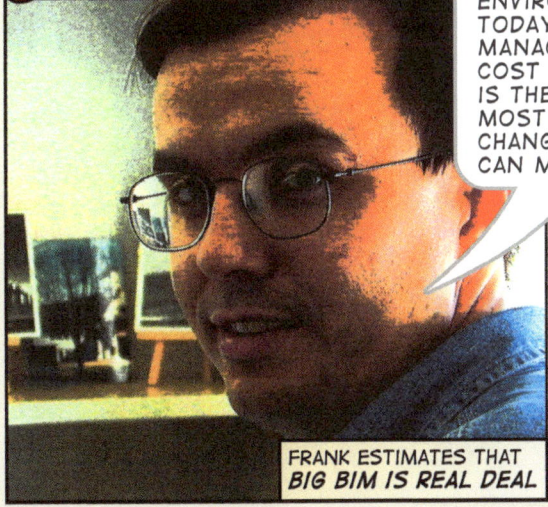

OCTOBER 1998

> COSTS IS THE PRIMARY CONSTRAINT ON THE BUILT ENVIRONMENT TODAY. MANAGEMENT OF COST CONSTRAINTS IS THE SINGLE MOST IMPORTANT CHANGE THAT YOU CAN MAKE.

FRANK ESTIMATES THAT *BIG BIM IS REAL DEAL*

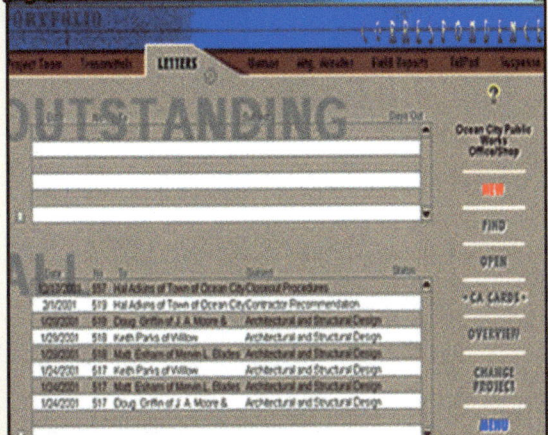

MAY 1999

FINITH DIVES INTO *INTEGRATED DATA*

Goals and philosophy that drive the process.

- Help others understand and believe in the change.

- Align with others focused on similar goals.

- Explore new and evolving technology.

- Design, test, and apply tools to manage information.

- Use innovation as a management tool.

- Explore new roles and understand new viewpoints.

- Build an environment for positive change.

- Involve your supply chain in decision-making.

- Confirm decisions to create future value - Do not track blame.

WHAT IS BIM?
FACT BASED DECISION MAKING

2000

IN THE SIXTH CENTURY BC, LAO TSE SAID—"MEN IN BUSINESS AFFAIRS COME NEAR PERFECTION, THEN FAIL. IF THEY WERE AS ATTENTIVE AT THE END AS AT THE BEGINNING, THEIR BUSINESS WOULD SUCCEED."

We can fix these problems...

...BIG BIM is the solution

...and little bim enables the solution

Ocean City

- Know and understand how you work.

- "Fail-fast"...don't contine flawed processes

- Engage others earlier in more collaborative ways

- Maximize knowledge and productivity in front end of projects

- Adjust fee structures

- Manage liabilities

- Improve bottom line by improving productivity

JULY 2000

BIG BIM IN ACTION FOR *THE FIRST TIME!*

Building Information Model

Program Estimating System
Analysis/Concepts/Costs/Criteria/Comparables ProForma/Validation

Special Services
Designed to Maximize
Project Success

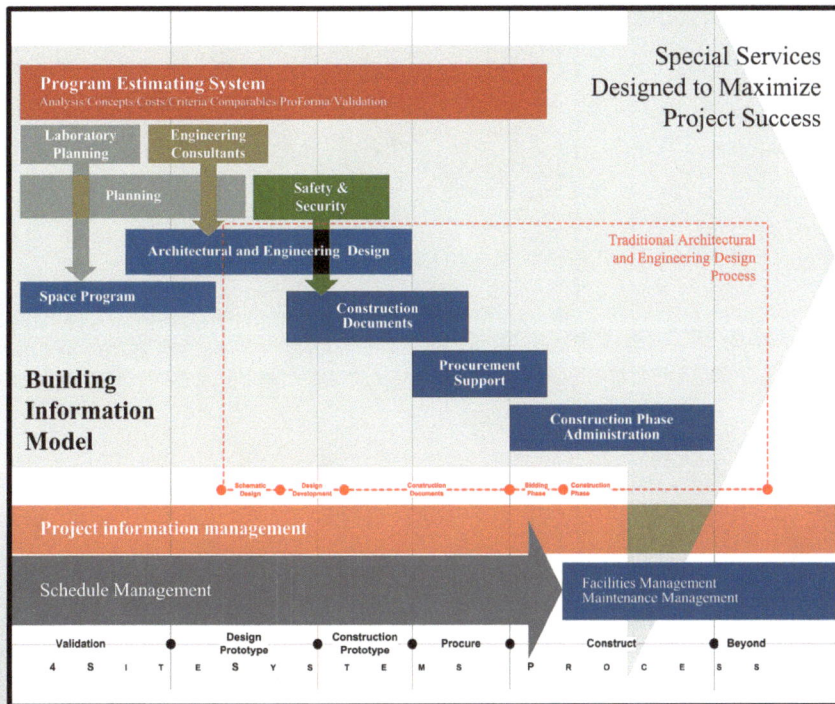

Laboratory Planning

Engineering Consultants

Planning

Safety & Security

Architectural and Engineering Design

Space Program

Construction Documents

Procurement Support

Traditional Architectural and Engineering Design Process

Construction Phase Administration

Schematic Design · Design Development · Construction Documents · Bidding Phase · Construction Phase

Project information management

Schedule Management

Facilities Management Maintenance Management

Validation	Design Prototype	Construction Prototype	Procure	Construct	Beyond

4 S I T E S Y S T E M S P R O C E S S

Clinging to old ways is no longer the best solution. Architects, builders and owners are making too many errors by being conservative. Forecasts must have greater accuracy. Become more flexible and plan with longer horizons.

The Owner determines needs, establishes the program and budget—in partnership with the constructor and designer.

The Constructor builds the project—in partnership with designer and owner. They expand the Facility Information Database and ensures that all sub-contractors, suppliers, and manufacturers adhere to guidelines and the project contract.

The Designer prototypes the solution—in partnership with the builder and owner. They manage the Facility Information Database. They confirm requirements through simulations, analysis, code and program confirmation, schedule, financial feasibility, and construction analysis.

Save time & money

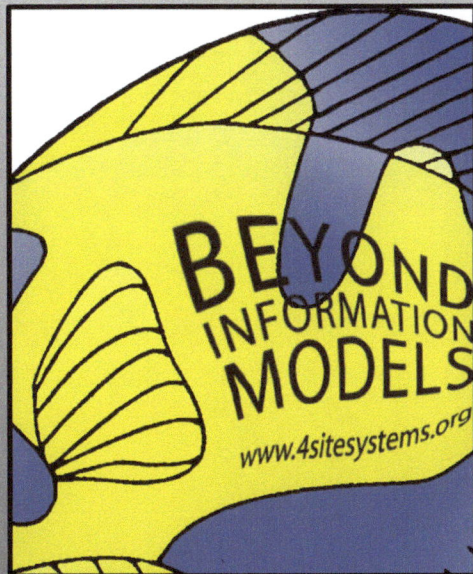

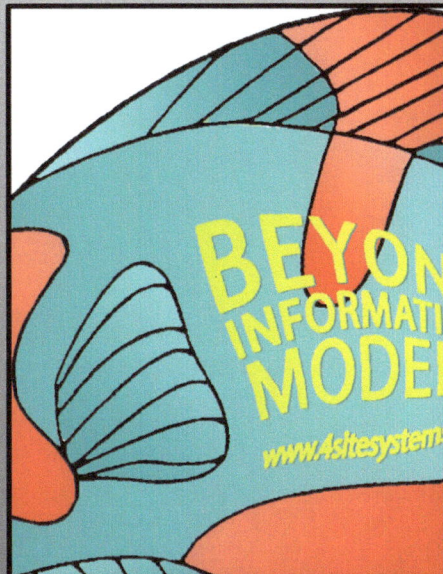

Poor documentation, cost overruns, and other problems happen because traditional management is not effective.

BEYOND INFORMATION MODELS
www.4sitesystems.org

BEYOND INFORMATION MODEL
www.4sitesystems

Find new and innovative ways to communicate your message.

MAY 2001

FRANK BRINGING BIG BIM TO *THE WORLD OF SPORTS*

Baltimore

- Understand your process

- Learn to manage change

- Expand your vision of the world—and where you fit in the building industry

EXPLORE HOW YOU CAN USE BIM TO MAKE SURE IT NEVER HAPPENS AGAIN.

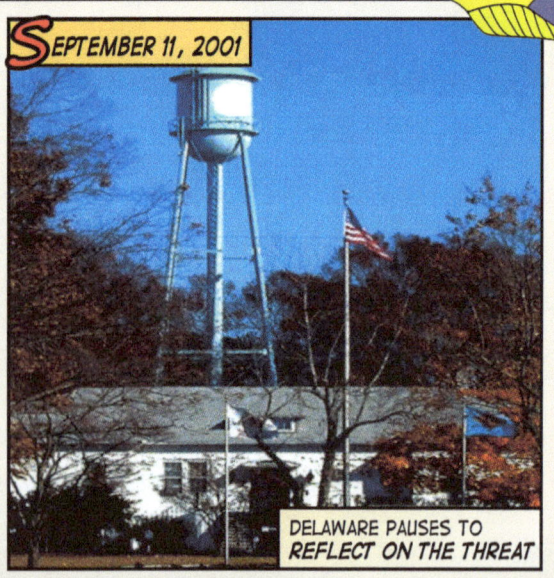

JULY 2001

ROBERT A. HUMPHREY SAID IT BEST WHEN HE SAID —"AN UNDEFINED PROBLEM HAS AN INFINITE NUMBER OF SOLUTIONS."

FINITH CAN EXPLAIN *BIG BIM TO ANYONE*

SEPTEMBER 11, 2001

DELAWARE PAUSES TO *REFLECT ON THE THREAT*

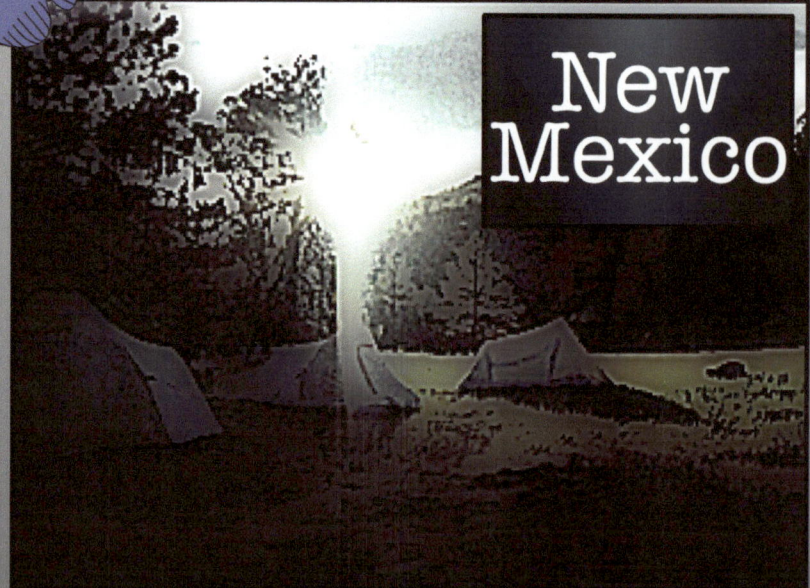

New Mexico

The process occurs within four continuous "phases" that represent the cycle of facilities—from cradle to cradle. The process fosters a holistic view of projects.

Initiate Phase—envision the project.

Design Phase—prototype with just the right data.

Construct Phase—adaptability is key.

Manage Phase—team BIM with Computer-Aided Facility Management (CAFM) to create long-term value.

Facility condition reports

Those that live with a building see problems well before anyone else. Use this forum to send the repair team notes of issues that you run across as you live in Sea Colony. Please be sure to give us enough information so that we can find the problem or talk to you to start the process of getting it resolved.

"Escrow Analysis"
sea colony trial   powered by ZOHO Sheet   Save As Excel

Asset	Location	Orig date	Last repair	Est life	Est repair date	Est cost	Escrow current	Escrow annual
balconies	unit 1005	10/05/2005	10/07/06	15	06/15/10	3000	1000	1000
	unit 4007	10/05/2005	10/07/06	15	06/15/10	2500	1000	750
	unit 2400	10/05/2005	10/07/06	15	06/15/10	4000	1000	1500
	unit 3400	10/05/2005	10/07/06	15	06/15/10	10000	4500	2500
condensing	unit 1005	10/05/2005	10/07/06	15	06/15/10	3000	1000	1000
	unit 4007	10/05/2005	10/07/06	15	06/15/10	2500	1000	750
	unit 2400	10/05/2005	10/07/06	15	06/15/10	4000	1000	1500
	unit 3400	10/05/2005	10/07/06	15	06/15/10	10000	4500	2500
						39000	15000	11500

SUSTAIN YOUR ASSETS
DEVELOP PLANS COLLABORATIVELY

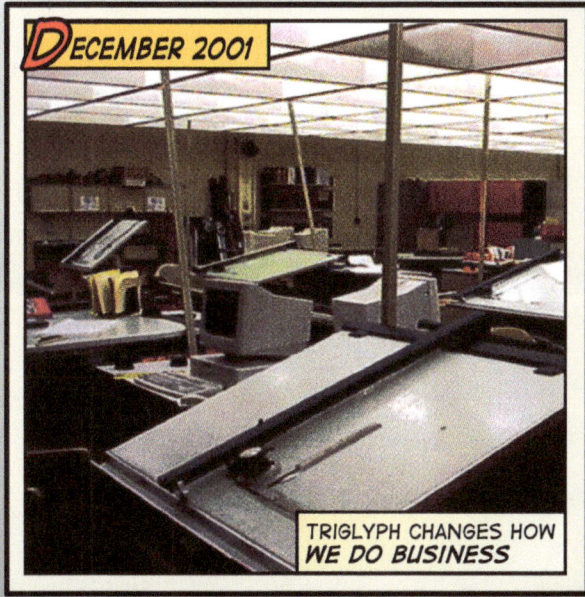

DECEMBER 2001

TRIGLYPH CHANGES HOW WE DO BUSINESS

Milwaukee

- Facilities are business **ASSETS**
- Link facilities to mission
- Cradle to cradle

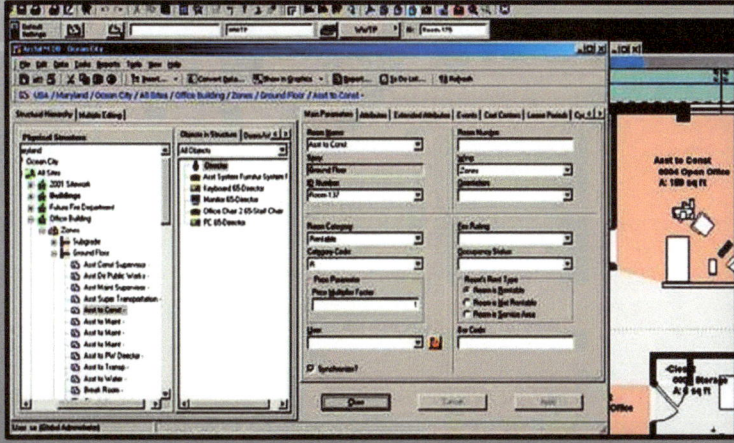

- **Critical** - envision the project properly
- Align concept, scope, and budget
- Define success at the beginning

Unchallenged beliefs cause a repeat errors. They sub-optimize how you do business. Apply creativity to business and become a strong force in the economy.

2002

> *"Having the details to make early decisions paid off... We were on track to make some expensive mistakes."*

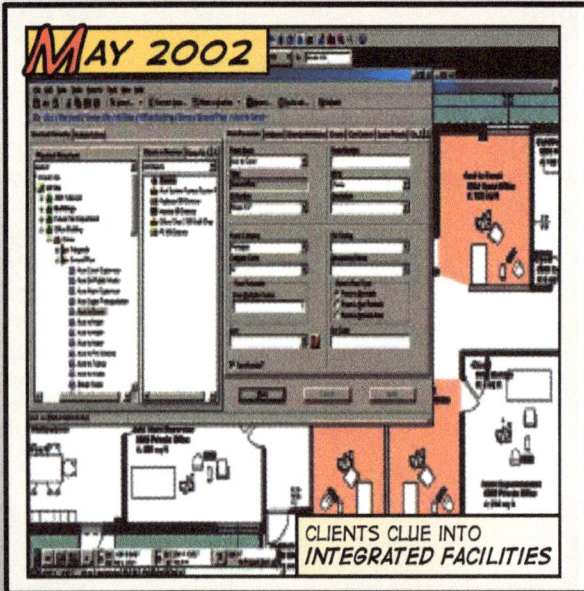

MAY 2002

CLIENTS CLUE INTO
INTEGRATED FACILITIES

THIS I BELIEVE ABOUT INTEGRATED PRACTICE:

- DESIGN IS PART OF EVERYTHING.

- THE PROCESS IS MANAGED BY CONSTRAINTS.

- DESIGN AND IMPLEMENTATION CAN AND SHOULD WORK IN PARALLEL.

- EARLY DECISIONS AFFECT THE QUALITY OF OUTCOMES.

- LEGACY SYSTEMS MUST NOT OVERSHADOW GOOD BUSINESS DECISIONS.

- WE CAN DEFINE OBJECTIVES THAT CREATE VALUE FOR EVERYONE.

- COMMUNICATION AND SHARING BUILD STRONG PROJECT TEAMS.

- WE ARE CRITICAL TO CLIENTS' SUCCESS.

The acronym BIM was coined in early 2002 to describe virtual design, construction,

Improve outcomes

- ✳ Capture existing assets - *once and for all*
- ✳ Better project $ long term
- ✳ Improve predictability
- ✳ Local support

- Constantly explore and evaluate new technologies

- Understand and use the core tools

- Ability to synthesize is critical - experience counts

> *"The benefits of the process are truly amazing...the process eliminates tedious, repetitious tasks."*

JULY 2002

15

CHICAGO AND SALISBURY
WORK IN PHILADELPHIA

bim (lower case) represents applications-focused topics; i.e., ArchiCad, Bentley, and Revit are bim tools.

BIM (upper case) is the management of information and the complex relationships between the social and technical resources that represent the complexity, collaboration, and interrelationships of organizations and the environment.

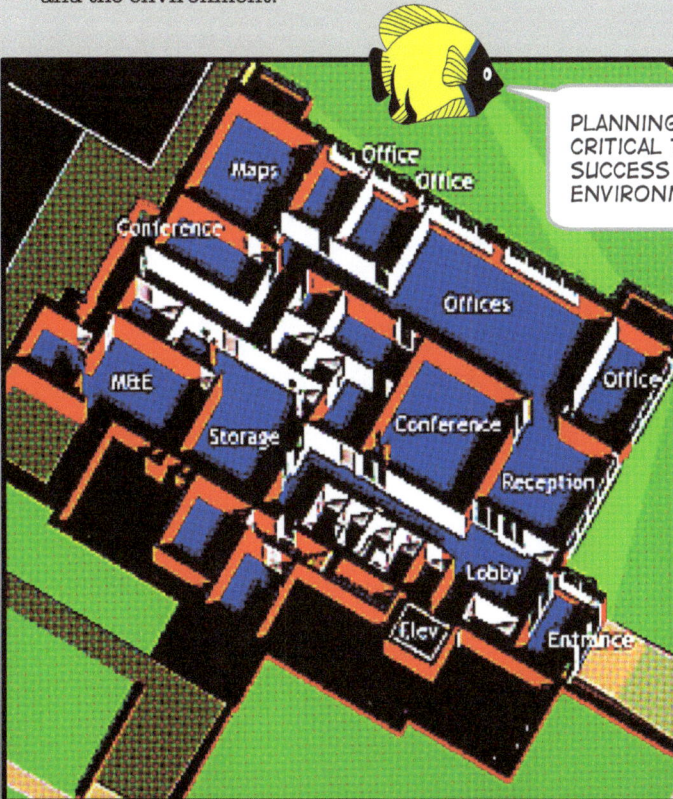

PLANNING IS CRITICAL TO SUCCESS IN THIS ENVIRONMENT.

Denton MD

BIM is a very different approach that aligns knowledge and ability—to reduce mundane and repetitive tasks. It works best for those that can synthesize complex data. It reduces workflow problems...and focuses on DESIGN.

ADVANCED IMAGERY + DETAILS = CERTAINTY
TRY YOUR IDEAS IN THE MODEL...

bim is not...

BIM is not CAD. BIM is not 3D. BIM is not application oriented.

BIM is managing information to improve understanding. In the traditional process, you lose information as you move from phase to phase. You make decisions when information becomes available, not at the optimal time. BIM is much different.

BY MINIMIZING MUNDANE TASKS...BIM REDUCES ERRORS.

⚠ WARNING

THIS IS NOT A BUILDING INFORMATION MODEL. DOCUMENT MUST BE COORDINATED MANUALLY BEFORE USE.

PROJECTS THAT DO NOT USE BIM SHOULD BE REQUIRED TO BE LABELED TO PROTECT THE PUBLIC FROM HARM.

- **BIM is not a single building model or a single database.**
- **BIM is not a replacement for people.**
- **BIM will not automate you out of existence.**
- **BIM is not perfect.**

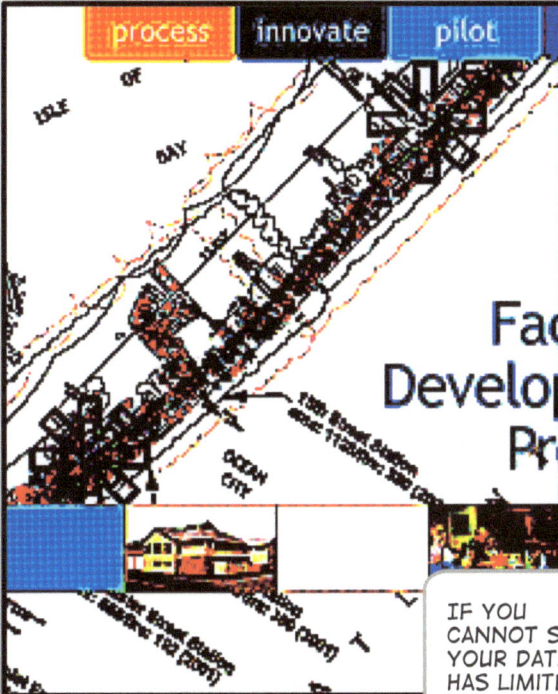

YOUR MODELING TOOL IS A HIGHLY PERSONAL DECISION. BECOME COMFORTABLE IN CREATING IN WHICHEVER TOOL YOU CHOOSE.

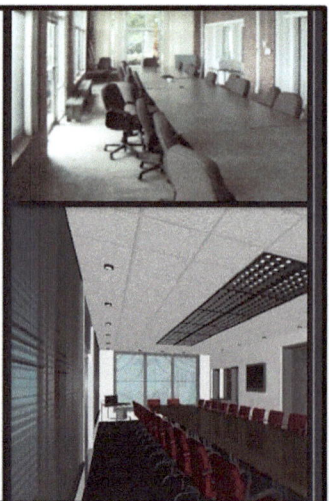

		Thermal Comfort - Compliance	1
		Thermal Comfort - Permanent Monitoring System	1
		Daylight & Views - Daylight for 50% of Spaces	1
		Daylight & Views - Daylight for 75% of Spaces	1
		Daylight & Views - Views for 45% of Spaces	1
		Daylight & Views - Views for 90% of Spaces	1
		Contemporary IAQ Practice	1
		Green Cleaning - Entryway Systems	1
		Green Cleaning - Isolation of Janitorial Closets	1
		Green Cleaning - Low Environmental Impact Cleaning Policy	1
	Credit 10.4	**Green Cleaning** - Low Environmental Impact Pest Management Policy	1
Yes	Credit 10.5	**Green Cleaning** - Low Environmental Impact Pest Management Policy	1
Yes	Credit 10.6	**Green Cleaning** - Low Environmental Impact Cleaning Equipment Policy	1

Innovation and Design Process		(Credits: 5 / Possible : 0 / No: 0)		5 Points
Yes	Credit 1.1	Historic Reclamation	1	
Yes	Credit 1.2	Chesapeake Bay Water Quality Improvement	1	
Yes	Credit 1.3	Crime Prevention Through Environmental Design	1	
Yes	Credit 1.4	Integrated Project Delivery Processes	1	
Yes	Credit 2	LEED Accredited Professional	1	

Project Totals	(Credits: 61 / Possible : 16 / No: 5)	85 Points
	LEED Gold: 61 Points	

SUSTAINABILITY
SAVE AND REUSE WHERE PRACTICAL - THINK LONG TERM

Is there a problem?

I know what the problem is, but I don't know how to fix it.

I can handle the problem as long as I work at it.

Managing the problem is part of my normal life.

2003

The convergence of BIM and the sustainability ethic offers an opportunity to engage the spectrum of building and project types in a richer way.

Texas

JULY 2003

Accepted methods aren't **acceptable** anymore.

Traditional Process

Virtual Collaboration Process

Portfolio Management

Project Delivery

Asset and Property Management

SAN ANTONIO IS HOT *FOR BIG BIM*

We are in a crisis

- We spend too much & get too little for our efforts

- We make too many decisions at the wrong time...with too little information

- Construction industry is inefficient and wastes resources

- We have the tools to change...

RIGHT NOW

Be a leader in a more productive and sustainable future

JULY 2003

19

AS-BUILT MODELS NEVER *SLEEP IN SEATTLE*

Seattle

It is not enough to have a good idea. Only when you act and implement can you make innovation happen day in and day out.

BIM OBJECTS SIMULATE REAL LIFE. DECISION MAKING DATA IS INCLUDED TO SPEED THE PROCESS.

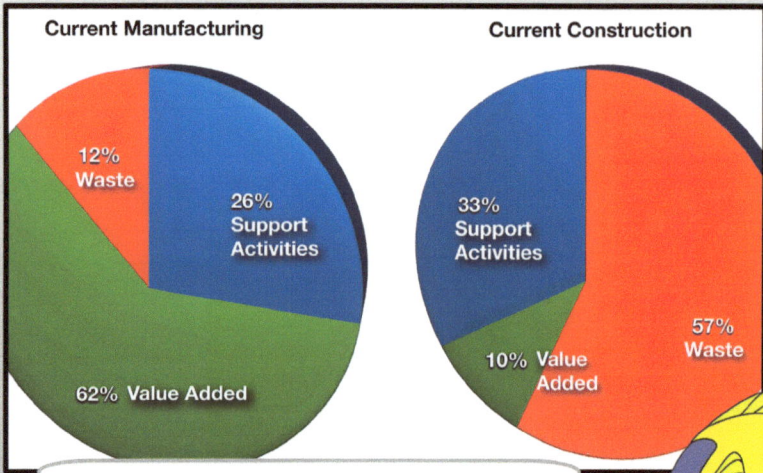

CAPTURE INFORMATION
USE YOUR $ EFFICIENTLY

MORNING TALK
INDIAN SHOP

FINITH IN NEW MEXICO
SEEKING BIG BIM

Current Manufacturing

- 26% Support Activities
- 12% Waste
- 62% Value Added

Current Construction

- 33% Support Activities
- 57% Waste
- 10% Value Added

Construction Industry Opportunity

57% waste less 26% waste =		31%
(Source CII & LCI 2004)		
Worldwide Construction	=	$4.8T
USA Construction	=	$1.3T
(Source ENR)		

31% x $1.3T = $400B
Annual savings by reducing construction process waste to industrial levels

WHY IS BUILDING INDUSTRY PRODUCTIVITY IN DECLINE? COULD IT BE THAT SOME HAVE NOT BEEN WILLING TO REALLY CHANGE?

BEGIN WITH A VISION AND HIRE PEOPLE THAT "GET IT"

Focus= People

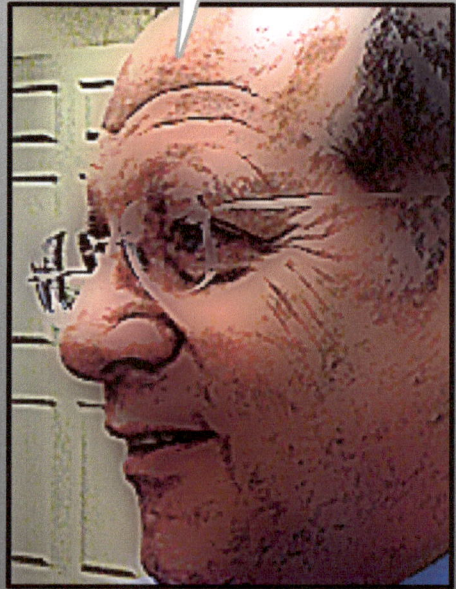

Why has the building industry computerized if there is no productivity gain? Other industries adapted to the changes and have improved the quality and effectiveness of their products. The building industry needs to change.

MARCH 2004

FOCUS ON MANAGING PROJECTS TO GET THE RIGHT INFORMATION TO THE RIGHT PLACE AT THE RIGHT TIME.

OHIO ROCKS FOR *BIG BIM*

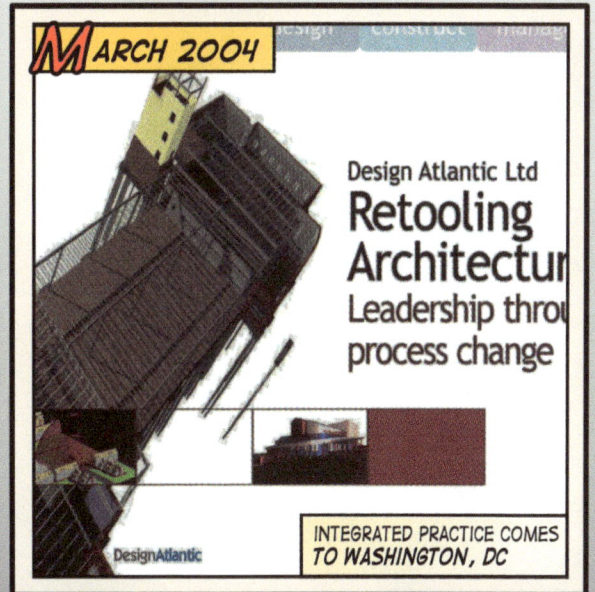

Cleveland

- *'Barreling ahead without a plan'* will work against you

- Right information for each stage while planning future needs

- *'Normal'* bim model

MARCH 2004

Design Atlantic Ltd
Retooling Architectur
Leadership throu
process change

DesignAtlantic

INTEGRATED PRACTICE COMES
TO WASHINGTON, DC

2004

Washington DC

Look at "first principles" that drive your business. Define business goals. Evaluate your capabilities and understand how customers will perceive the value of the change.

If you can describe something, it can be captured. If it can be captured, you can define its relationship to other knowledge.

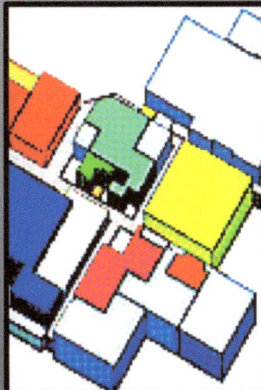

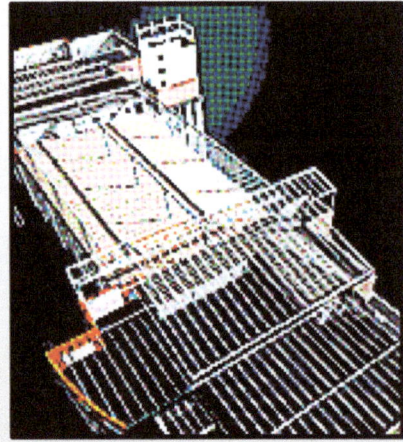

The greatest benefits come when we share data with others —both in the design and construction process.

DETAILED ANALYSIS OF PROJECTS STARTS AT THE BEGINNING OF PROJECTS. DECISIONS CAN THEN BE MADE WITH DEPENDABLE FACTS.

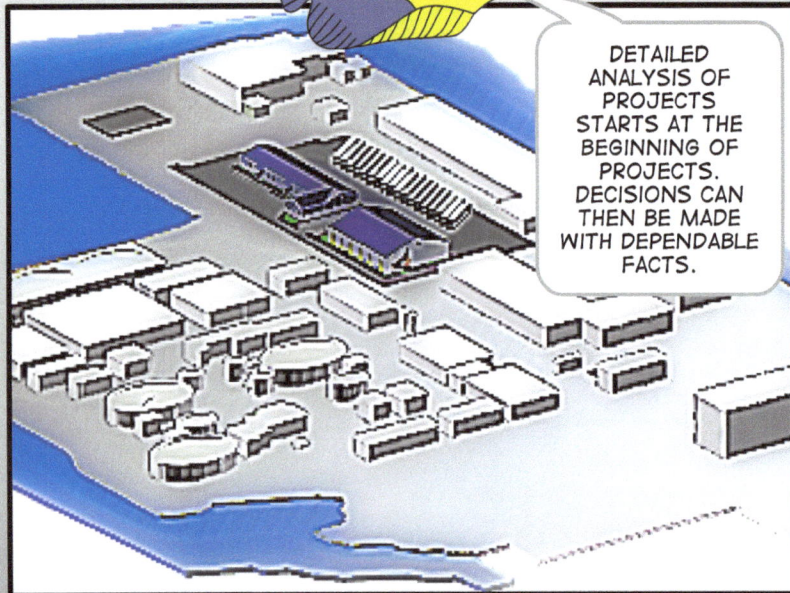

APRIL 2004

BIG BIM PROTECTS THE *CHESAPEAKE BAY*

Chesapeake Bay

Files for this project

Sort by
- Date and time
- A–Z
- File size

TUESDAY, 16 OCTOBER

sea colony.ifc
— trial ifc file
by Finith Jernigan in Interoperable files 1726K   Upload a new version   Edit

DAC-VA-DESIGN-SUBLOGO.dwg
— Sample dwg
by Finith Jernigan in CADD Document 93K   Upload a new version   Edit

Test1.xml
— GBS xml file
by Finith Jernigan in Interoperable files 53K   Upload a new version   Edit

sea colony test.pln
— Green Building Studio test file
by Finith Jernigan in Archicad files 1497K   Upload a new version   Edit

spalled concrete.gsm
— spalled concrete object
by Finith Jernigan in Library objects 7K   Upload a new version   Edit

THURSDAY, 5 JULY

4sitesystems BIM.pdf
4SiteSystems overview
by Finith Jernigan in Documents 5648K   Upload a new version   Edit

project delivery checklist.doc
4SiteSystems project delivery checklist

Categories

All files

Archicad files
CADD Document
Documents
Graphics
Interoperable files
Library objects
Pictures

CENTRAL ARCHIVE
DATA WHEN NEEDED - ACCESSIBLE & IN YOUR PREFERRED FORMAT

Files for this project

Upload a file

TUESDAY, 16 OCTOBER

sea colony.ifc
trial ifc file
by Finith Jernigan in Interoperable files 1726K   Upload a new version   Edit

DAC-VA-DESIGN-SUBLOGO.dwg
Sample dwg
by Finith Jernigan in CADD Document 93K   Upload a new version   Edit

Test1.xml
GBS xml file
by Finith Jernigan in Interoperable files 5.3K   Upload a new version   Edit

sea colony test.pln
Green Building Studio test file
by Finith Jernigan in Archicad files 1497K   Upload a new version   Edit

spalled concrete.gsm
spalled concrete object
by Finith Jernigan in Library objects 7K   Upload a new version   Edit

THURSDAY, 5 JULY

4sitesystems BIM.pdf
4SiteSystems overview
by Finith Jernigan in Documents 5648K   Upload a new version   Edit

project delivey checklist.doc
4SiteSystems project delivery checklist

Sort by
- Date and time
- A-Z
- File size

Categories
All files
Archicad files
CADD Document

BIM MODEL SERVERS WILL SOME DAY ARCHIVE AND COORDINATE YOUR FACILITY DATA. UNTIL THEN YOU NEED A FILE STORAGE AND SHARING STRATEGY.

CENTRAL ARCHIVE
DATA WHEN NEEDED - ACCESSIBLE & IN YOUR PREFERRED FORMAT

APRIL 2004

ATLANTIC CITY BETS *ON BIG BIM*

Use BIM at the beginning of projects. Make every possible decision, as early as possible. Conceive the design using building information models from the beginning.

BIM IS A GREAT TOOL FOR RENOVATING AND RESTORING HISTORIC BUILDINGS.

Start with five principles:

Clear and open communication is the first priority.

Optimize working practices, methods, and behaviors.

Build structures that capture everything, then share the information.

Use knowledge to eliminate the mundane and speed decisions.

The right information, at the right time, to those who decide.

IMPLEMENTING BIM WITHOUT CHANGING THE TRADITIONAL PROCESSES IS FRAUGHT WITH PROBLEMS.

London

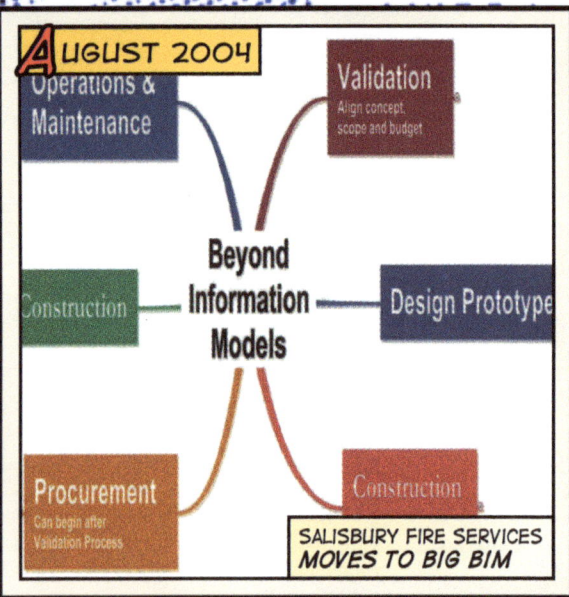

JULY 2004

VICKSBURG LIGHTS UP *FOR BIG BIM*

AUGUST 2004

Operations & Maintenance

Validation
Align concept, scope and budget

Construction

Beyond Information Models

Design Prototype

Procurement
Can begin after Validation Process

Construction

SALISBURY FIRE SERVICES *MOVES TO BIG BIM*

Vicksburg

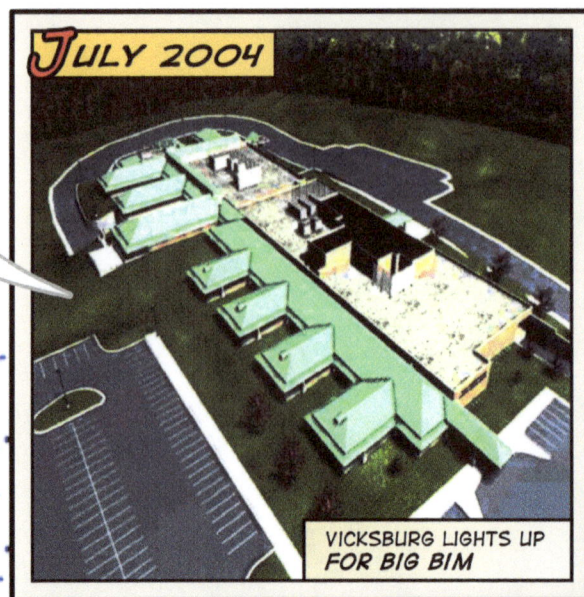

WRITER MIGUEL DE CERVANTES' INSIGHT, "FOREWARNED IS FOREARMED," STILL RINGS TRUE OVER ONE HUNDRED AND NINETY YEARS LATER.

SEPTEMBER 2004

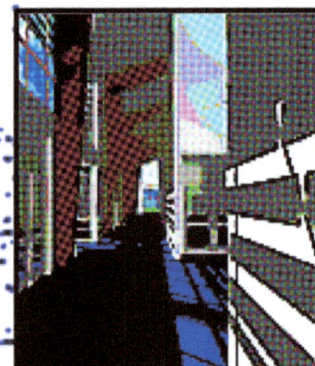

FIGHTING THREATS *WITH BIG BIM*

OCTOBER 2004

FRANK SAVES THE SEAS *WITH BIG BIM*

If an industrial designer creates a product that cannot economically be manufactured, packaged, and sold, what happens? Is the same true for architects?

"PEOPLE NEED TO BE REMINDED MORE OFTEN THAN THEY NEED TO BE INSTRUCTED." —DR. SAMUEL JOHNSON

Done correctly, BIG BIM changes how everyone looks at our world

2005

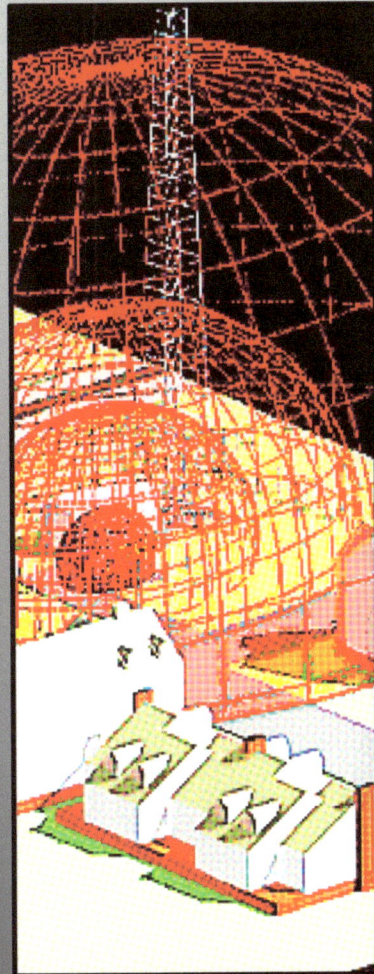

With the correct strategy and vision for the project, the phases that follow become easier to manage and more successful.

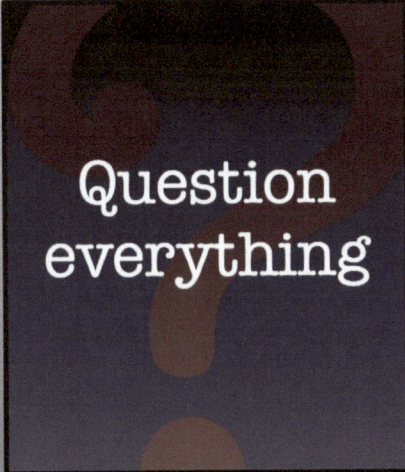

MARCH 2005

FINITH ON THE TRAIL OF *BIG BIM IN LONDON*

The best approach is to be wary. Question everything, no matter how plausible or enticing the message.

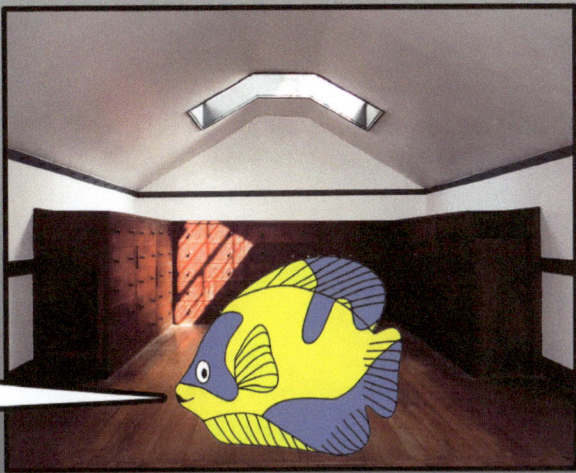

Question everything

IDENTIFY AND MANAGE CONSTRAINTS TO MANAGE THE PERFORMANCE OF ANY COMPLEX PROCESS.

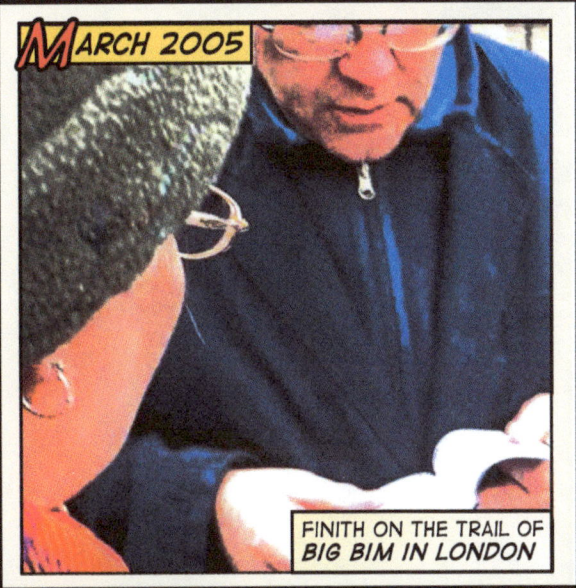

DOWNSTREAM USES
NEW USES FOR YOUR INFORMATION

WHEN YOU HAVE A MODEL, YOU HAVE THE ABILITY TO ANALYZE YOUR DESIGN LIKE NEVER BEFORE.

MARCH 2005

LOOKING AT WORLDWIDE *SCHOOLS IN SAN ANTONIO*

> "Our last $1 million project was a heck of a lot more work and effort than this $9 million project.
>
> *It was a lot of work before, ...this was much easier."*
>
> William Gordy, Deputy Fire Chief

BIM and process integration may be the ultimate step in moving Owners from the "throw it away and start over" approach to information.

JUNE 2005

BILL ENLIGHTENED *BY BIG BIM*

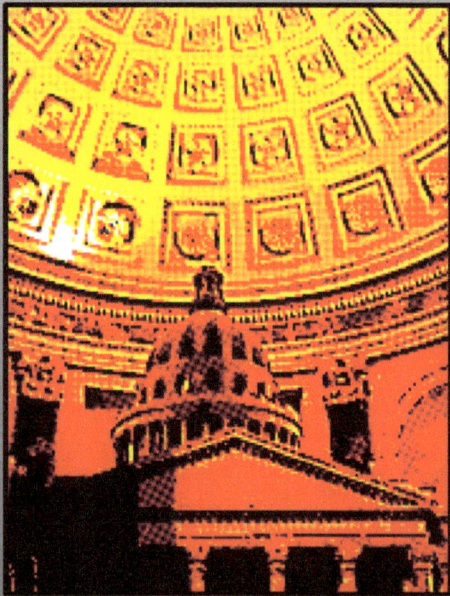

Confusion creeps into the discussion of BIM for a variety of reasons. The complexity of the subject and self-interest leads to many of the misunderstandings. Sometimes people are more interested in making a sale than in the truth. The battle for dominance among vendors leads to messages designed to put products in the best light and sometime reality gets lost in the hype. The confusion is usually unintentional, but sometimes not, so beware.

Helsinki

Find common objectives, share information and use open and honest business standards. Be a leader in the process.

JULY 2005

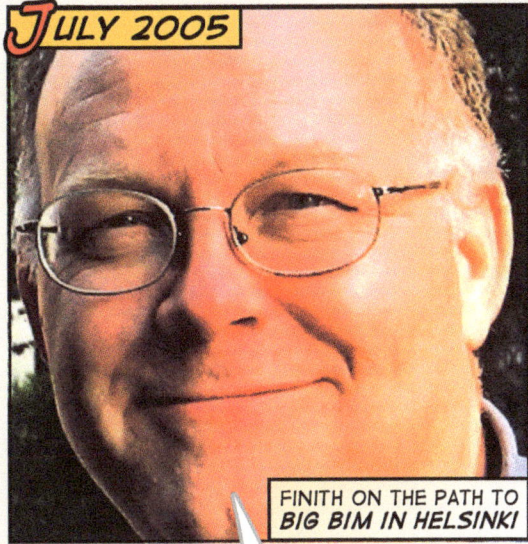

FINITH ON THE PATH TO *BIG BIM IN HELSINKI*

OWNERS WANT PROJECTS TO BE UNDER CONTROL. THEY WANT TO KNOW WHERE THEY ARE GOING. TECHNOLOGY GIVES YOU THE TOOLS TO MAKE IT HAPPEN.

Levels of Detail

Type 1 Digital Repository	Type 2 Concept Vision	Type 3 Design Prototype	Type 4 Construction Prototype	Type 5 Construction Model	Type 6 Management Model
LOD 1 Data + GiS	LOD 2 3D Shell	LOD 3 Shell +	LOD 4 Layering in Data	LOD 5 Visualization & Analysis	LOD 6 Maintain & Update

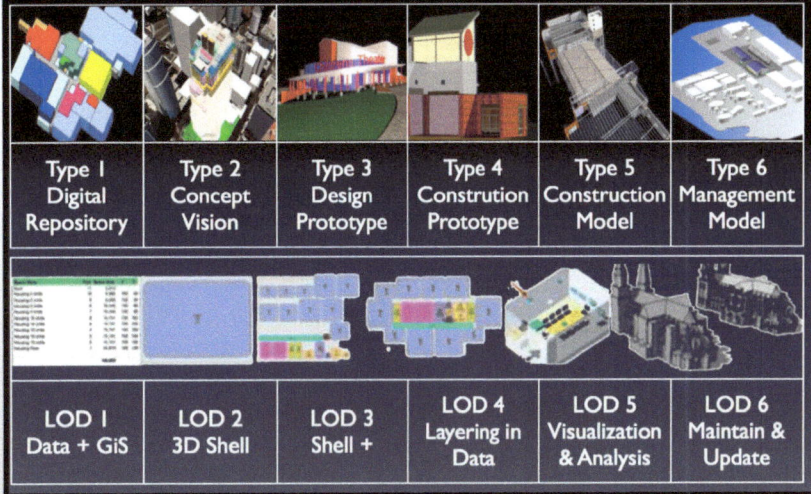

Build models step-by-step, planning for the future.

FAILURES HAPPEN BECAUSE OF SMALL, EASILY CORRECTABLE FLAWS AT THE BEGINNING.

AUGUST 2005

Design Atlantic Ltd
Strategic Planning Group

DesignAtlantic

PENNSYLVANIA FIREFIGHTERS *PLAN WITH BIG BIM*

Milestones (Today is 16 October)

KNOW WHERE TO FIND THE ANSWERS
ONE PLACE FOR ALL TO UNDERSTAND

Atlanta

2006

Use BIM tools to integrate decision-making with owner's business processes.

Business Process Planning

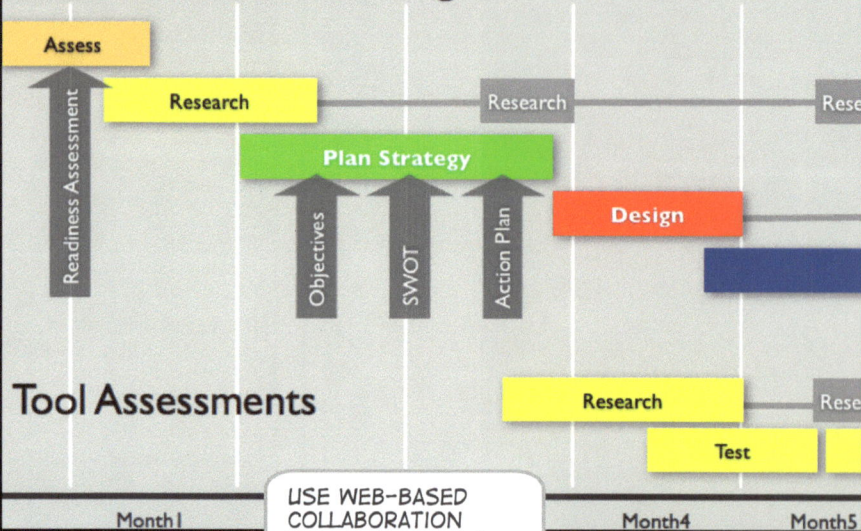

Assess				
	Research		Research	Rese
		Plan Strategy		
			Design	

Readiness Assessment
Objectives
SWOT
Action Plan

Tool Assessments

Research		Rese
Test		

Month1   Month4   Month5

USE WEB-BASED COLLABORATION TOOLS FROM DAY ONE. MAKE COMMUNICATIONS CLEAR AND SIMPLE.

A systems approach to design and construction underpins Integrated Project Delivery.

The Carolinas

MARCH 2006

WITH HARD WORK, YOU CAN KEEP UP WITH THE TOOLS THAT ARE DEVELOPING EVERY DAY.

FRANK EXPLORES *BIG BIM IN S. CAROLINA*

MAY 2006

BIG BIM GOES TO *A MARYLAND BEACH*

SEPTEMBER 2006

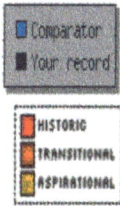

Team working
Respect for people
Outcomes
Communication
Values
IT Tools
Retention
Managing Risk
Logistics
Managing Value
Health, safety and environment
Payment
Efficiency

Comparator
Your record

HISTORIC
TRANSITIONAL
ASPIRATIONAL

FINITH FOCUSES BIG BIM *ON RESTON, VIRGINIA*

Design prototypes with "just enough" data to support the current need.

SEPTEMBER 11, 2006

STEP IN AND DO THE RIGHT THING AND, MAKE SURE THAT YOU THANK THOSE THAT SERVE AND PROTECT.

HONORING HEROES *WITH BIG BIM*

- New processes - new risks

- Do not allow tools to replace professional judgment

Day-to-day focus

- Predesign decision-making.
- Systems approach to design.
- Manage constraints.
- Free and open communications.
- Adapt to project needs.
- Optimize processes.
- Share information.

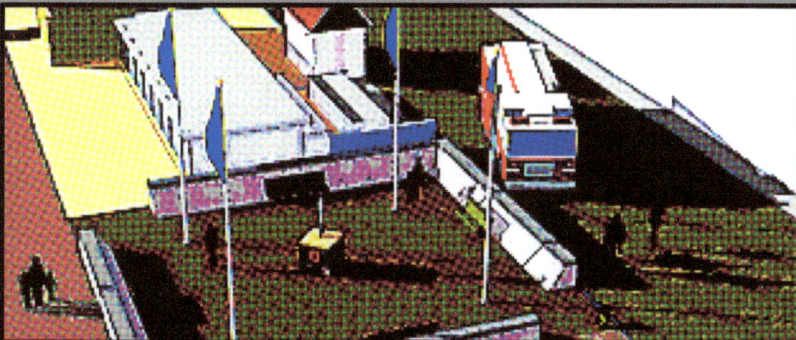

Community Activity Center
- NSF: 28,455
- GSF: 45,705
- Total Cost: $9,334,409
- Total Energy Use: 537,808 kWh
- Construction Start Date: Mar 2010
- Construction Duration 18 Months
- Building Type: 1.2.1 - Assembly
- LEEDS Rating: Gold
- Roof Runoff Total Area All

Scheme Cost
Project Name: Friends of Quonock School
Scheme Name: Promotional Concept

SITE WORK:	
BUILDING CONSTRUCTION COST	
Home Arts Museum	
Living History Shops	
Outdoor Performance Venue	
Community Activity Center	
TOTAL COST SITE/SCHEME	

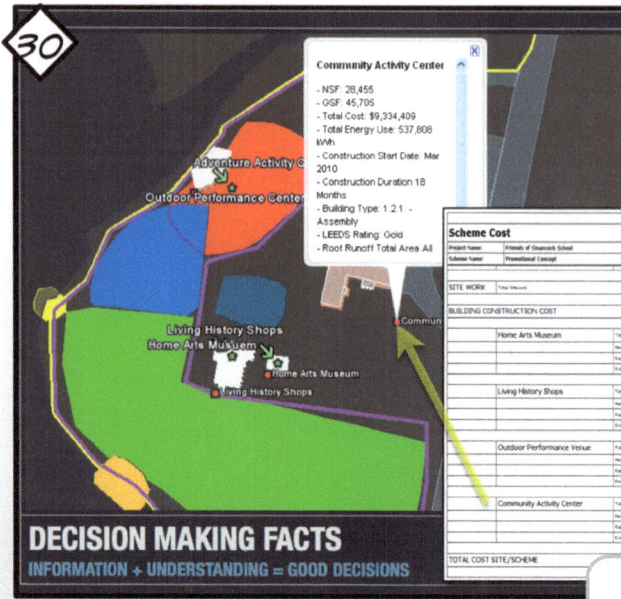

DECISION MAKING FACTS
INFORMATION + UNDERSTANDING = GOOD DECISIONS

30,000 SF & $4.5 million before validation

USE BIM TO MAKE SURE THAT YOUR PROJECTS START OFF ON THE RIGHT FOOT.

41,655 SF & $9.2 million after validation

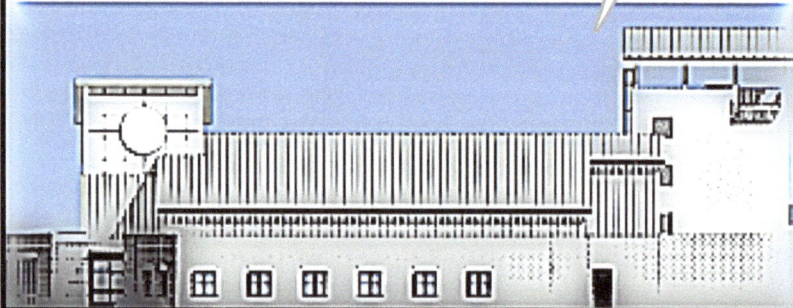

OCTOBER 2006

FIRE CHIEFS RESCUE BUDGET
WITH BIG BIM

Focus your creative energies on getting quality decisions early.

$752,000 ...under budget ...on schedule ...no claims

USE BIM TO INFORM EVERYONE ON THE JOB. WHEN PEOPLE KNOW WHAT IS GOING ON, THEY WORK BETTER.

OCTOBER 2006

BEYOND INFORMATION MODELS
www.4sitesystems.org

LAKE GENEVA STUDIES
HOW TO BIG BIM

NOVEMBER 2006

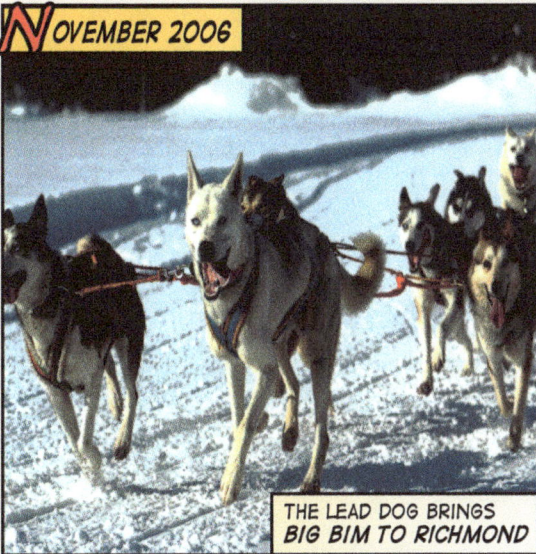

THE LEAD DOG BRINGS
BIG BIM TO RICHMOND

- Tailor the process to your firm

- Do not wait until someone else works everything out

- One-step at a time

Chicago

If you want people to follow standards, the standards must be simple.

We can fix the problems, with...

- Open and appropriate technology

- Full collaboration

- Information sharing

- Reusable digital information

Integrated practice offers benefits for firms of all shapes and sizes. The trick is to tailor the process, since 'one size does NOT fit all.'

Use email for noncritical communications only. Email does not support the level of communications and collaboration that integrated practice requires. Email permits too much uncertainty and too many things fall through the cracks.

- Tailor to your project's need

- **MUST** build these models accurately

- Take responsibility for entire effort

2007

Little stuff
over & over again

> AN EASY TO USE AND CLEAR COMMUNICATIONS PORTAL IS CRITICAL!

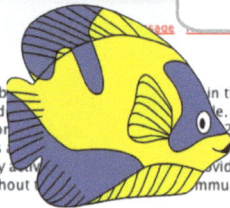

Focus on minimizing the "first-day" mistakes.

There is great value in early certainty.

| Overview | Messages | To-Do | Milestones | Writeboards | Chat | Files |

Project overview & activity

Whether you want a beach front condo with fab... ...in the ...nis community surrounded by picturesque lakes and lush land... ...le, beauty, and grace of quality homes to surf, sand, and fun for everyo... ...ools to lounge from, 34 tennis courts to challenge your skills as well as ... ...ics, a 17,000 square foot fitness and aquatics center, and family-friendly a... ...vide a complimentary beach shuttle to take you anywhere you need throughout ... ...mmunity.

Relax, unwind, and sink your feet in the sand while you experience Sea Colony – The Beautiful Beach and Tennis Resort.

Late & Upcoming Milestones

15 days late: *** Use milestones to track contract expiration/renewal*** (Sea Colony Phase II is responsible)

Due in the next 14 days

Tue	Wed	Thu	Fri	Sat	Sun	Mon
TODAY			19 Present to Board			
			26 Revise proposal/submit agreement			

MONDAY, 15 OCTOBER

Milestone	*** Use milestones to track contract expiration/renewal*** (Due 1 Oct)	Assigned to: Sea Colony Phase II
Message	Condition Index	Posted by Finith J.
Message	What should I post here?	Posted by Finith J.

A PORTAL TO CERTAINTY
REDUCE THE MYSTERY

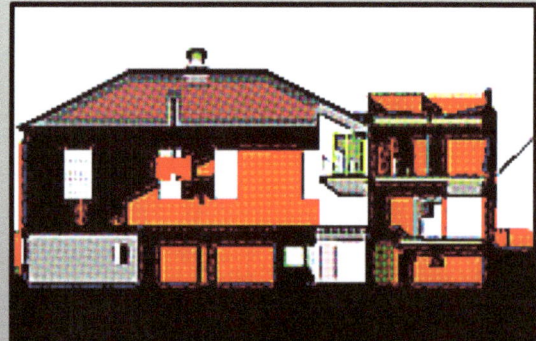

> "IT HAS LONG BEEN AN AXIOM OF MINE THAT THE LITTLE THINGS ARE INFINITELY THE MOST IMPORTANT." —SIR ARTHUR CONAN DOYLE

Common sense & good business

USE BIM TO STUDY HOW YOUR PROJECTS IMPACT ON CRITICAL AREAS.

New Jersey

Paris

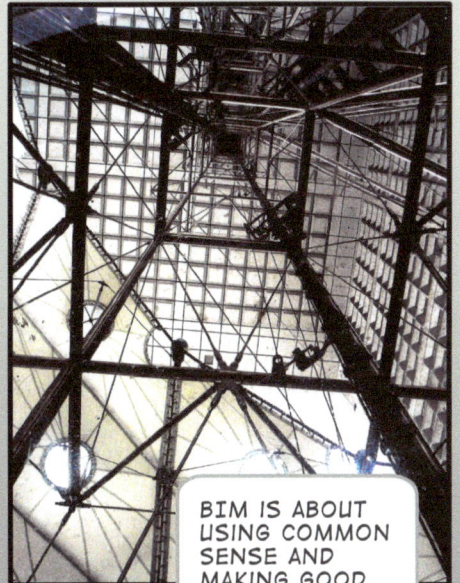

BIM IS ABOUT USING COMMON SENSE AND MAKING GOOD BUSINESS DECISIONS.

Change the focus from designing projects to getting certainty about projects.

FINITH SEARCHING FOR
BIG BIM IN PARIS

TURN AROUND CONCEPTS FOR NEW PROJECTS, FAST!

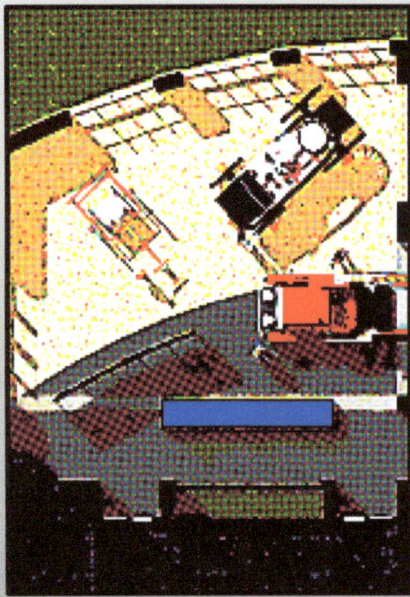

AGENCY CONSTRUCTION MANAGERS CONSISTENTLY SOLVE OWNER PROBLEMS. THE SAME IS WIDELY HELD TO BE TRUE FOR DESIGN/BUILDERS. IS THIS BECAUSE OWNERS TRUST THEM TO WORK IN THEIR BEST INTERESTS?

JUNE 2007

FINITH LOOKING FOR *BIG BIM IN LA*

BUILD CUSTOM OBJECTS FOR NEARLY ANYTHING YOU CAN IMAGINE.

34

Sea Colony Phase II

Overview | Messages | To-Do | Milestones | Writeboards | Chat | Files | People & Permissions | Search

All Messages

Expanded view | List view | Post a new message

MONDAY, 15 OCTOBER

Condition Index

Priorities for repairs and replacement are made based upon assessed condition index. Condition Index is based on a scale of 1 to 100, with 100 representing a new, defect-free asset or component.

——Scale——Rating——Recommendation——

- 86-100---Excellant---Routine maintenance
- 71-85---Very Good---Minor repairs needed
- 56-70---Good---------Moderate repairs needed
- 41-55---Fair---------Major repairs needed
- 26-40---Poor---------Replacement probable
- 11-25---Very Poor---Repacement needed
- 1-10---Failed------Replacement critical

Posted by Finith Jernigan in Construction | Edit | Post the first comment

What should I post here?

Messages is the place for such things as physical layouts, dimensions, sizes, address and tax ID numbers.

Posted by Finith Jernigan in Miscellaneous | Edit | Post the first comment

SUNDAY, 14 OCTOBER

Maintenance planning

Over the years, the association has found itself having to recreate drawings and

Categories Edit

All Messages
Construction
Design
Facilities Management
Files
Miscellaneous
Planning
Repairs-General
Repairs-Urgent

CONSISTENT RATINGS
MAKE PROCESS LESS SUBJECTIVE

TIE BUSINESS DECISIONS DIRECTLY TO THE BIM MODEL.

FINITH MEMORIALIZES **BIG BIM** LITTLE BIM

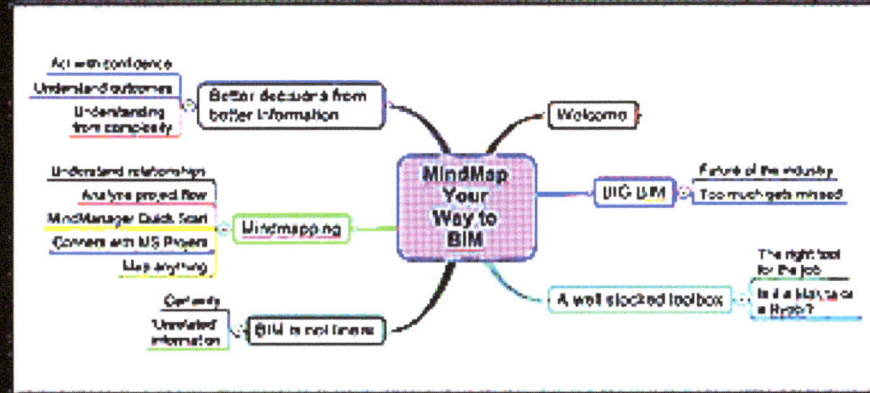

Maximize the effectiveness of projects.

- Minimize confusion and uncertainty.

- Be flexible and take the long view.

- Define success at the start.

- Solve problems as early as possible.

- Remove subjectivity.

- Involve everyone.

- Understand underlying needs.

- Avoid competition—work together.

- Take responsibility and make things happen.

Mindmapping is the ideal medium for documenting and communicating snippets of data. Organize information to find patterns. Brainstorm and see where your data takes you while keeping track and building a map of your project.

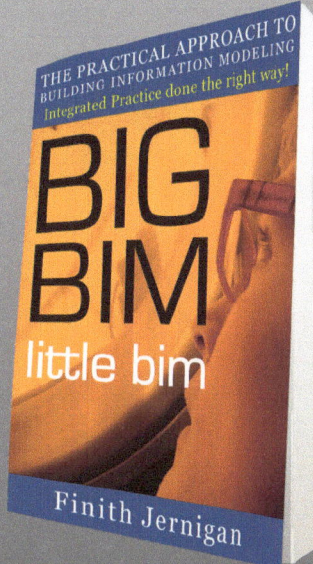

THE PRACTICAL APPROACH TO BUILDING INFORMATION MODELING
Integrated Practice done the right way!

BIG BIM little bim

Finith Jernigan

PLAN FOR FUTURE PUBLIC WORKS FACILITIES WITH A BIM MASTER MODEL.

- Arrive directly from many different points

- Avoided or missed questions =
  PROBLEMS LATER

- Clarity and simplicity

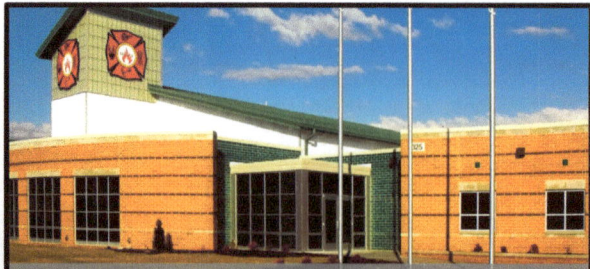

Do bim now—adapt and grow as tools improve

NOVEMBER 2007

JACK MAKES BIG BIM
REAL IN DELAWARE

There are always issues that fall outside of any system. You have to adapt and fill the holes. Perhaps someday someone will integrate everything into a truly functional system. For now, this remains the holy grail of integrated practice.

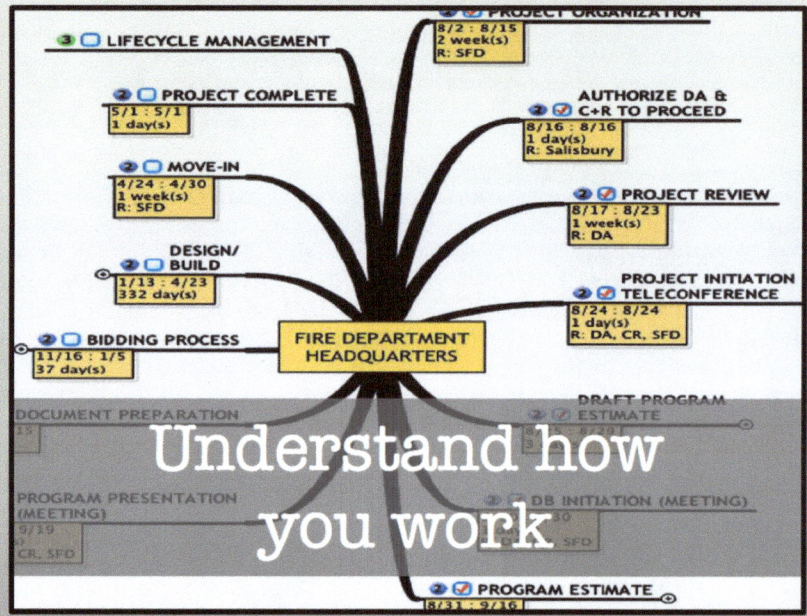

PROBLEMS WITH COMMUNICATIONS COME FROM THOSE WHO DO NOT UNDERSTAND THE PROCESS OR, FROM THOSE WHO UNDERSTAND IT AND CHOOSE TO CONTINUE WORKING THE WAY THEY ALWAYS WORKED.

3 ☐ LIFECYCLE MANAGEMENT

PROJECT ORGANIZATION
8/2 : 8/15
2 week(s)
R: SFD

2 ☐ PROJECT COMPLETE
5/1 : 5/1
1 day(s)

AUTHORIZE DA &
2 ☑ C+R TO PROCEED
8/16 : 8/16
1 day(s)
R: Salisbury

2 ☐ MOVE-IN
4/24 : 4/30
1 week(s)
R: SFD

2 ☑ PROJECT REVIEW
8/17 : 8/23
1 week(s)
R: DA

DESIGN/
BUILD
1/13 : 4/23
332 day(s)

PROJECT INITIATION
2 ☑ TELECONFERENCE
8/24 : 8/24
1 day(s)
R: DA, CR, SFD

2 ☐ BIDDING PROCESS
11/16 : 1/5
37 day(s)

FIRE DEPARTMENT HEADQUARTERS

DRAFT PROGRAM
2 ☑ ESTIMATE

DOCUMENT PREPARATION

PROGRAM PRESENTATION
(MEETING)

DB INITIATION (MEETING)

2 ☑ PROGRAM ESTIMATE
8/31 : 9/16

Understand how you work

DECEMBER 2007

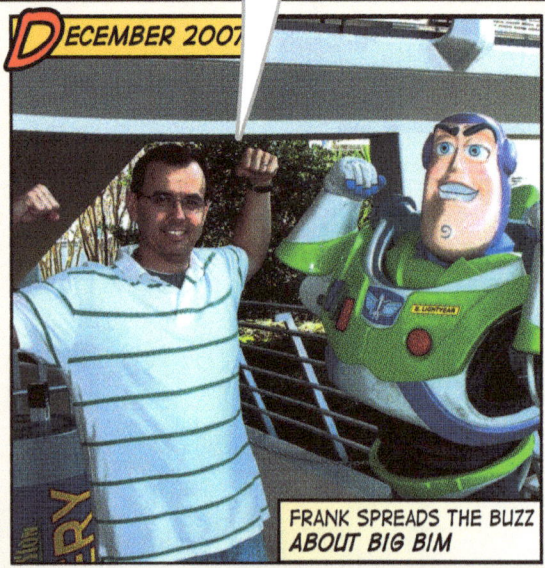

FRANK SPREADS THE BUZZ
ABOUT BIG BIM

Advanced imagery + details = CERTAINTY

BIG BIM is big picture industry transformation.

Advanced tools speed activities so much that business processes change.

2008

IT SEEMS SIMPLE. YOU HAVE TO START RIGHT.

RULES-BASED SYSTEMS DELIVER COMPLETE BIM FOR YOUR CLIENTS.

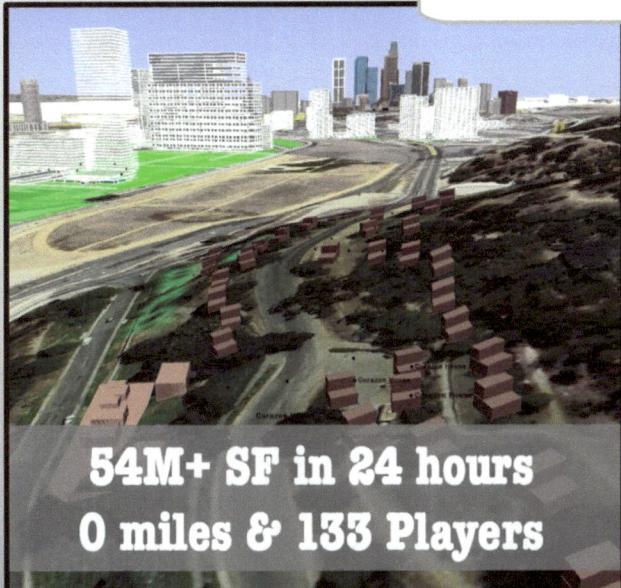

54M+ SF in 24 hours
0 miles & 133 Players

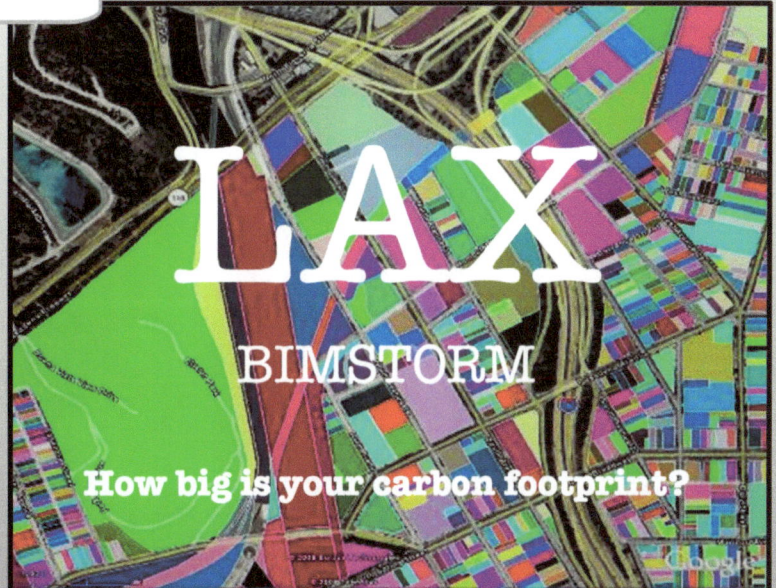

LAX
BIMSTORM
How big is your carbon footprint?

ADAPT OLD BUILDINGINGS TO NEW USES
GET CLIENTS THE MOST FOR THEIR MONEY

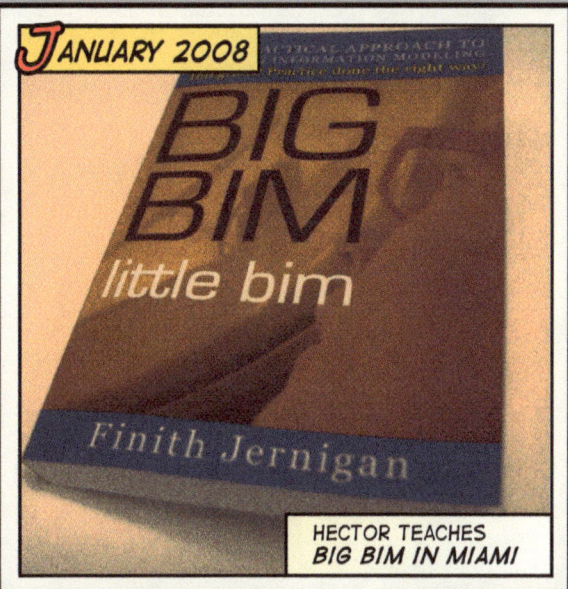

JANUARY 2008

BIG BIM
little bim
Finith Jernigan

HECTOR TEACHES
BIG BIM IN MIAMI

Tijuana - Corazón

BIG BIM BUILDS A *HOME IN TIJUANA*

HELPING PEOPLE *GET BIG BIM IN LOS ANGELES*

54M+ SF in 24 hours
0 miles & 133 Players

Tijuana

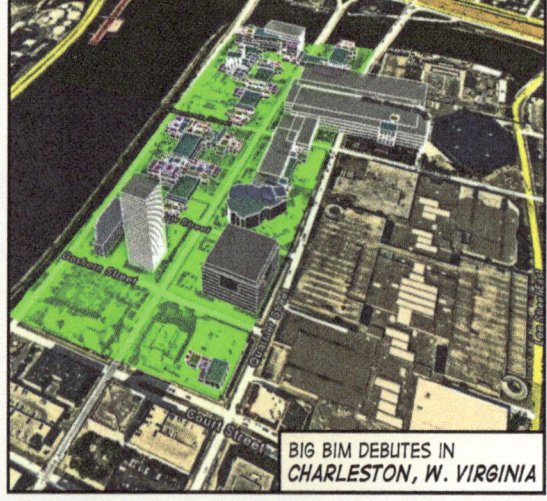

BIG BIM DEBUTES IN *CHARLESTON, W. VIRGINIA*

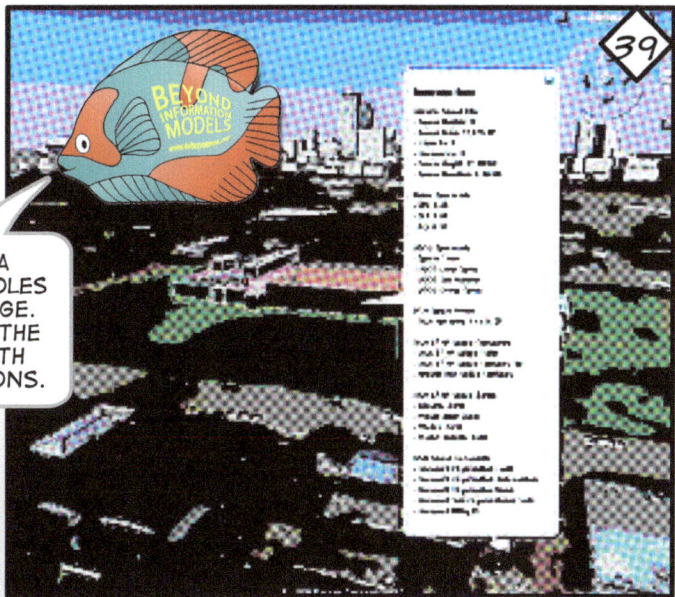

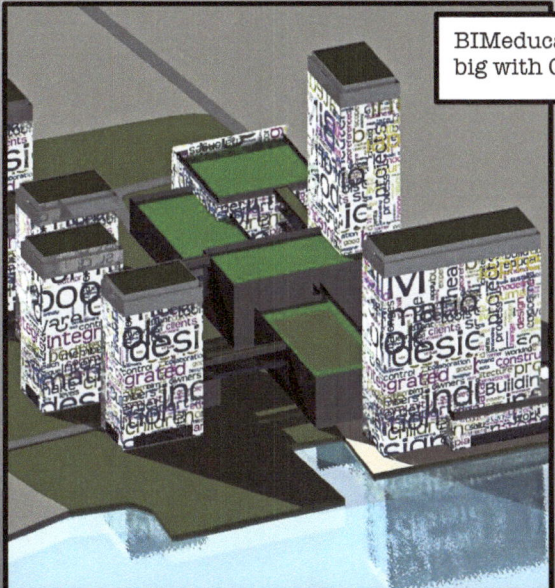

Create a safe and secure world using BIM and GiS.

THE AMERICAN INSTITUTE OF ARCHITECTS FOCUSES ON BIM AND INTEGRATED PRACTICE IN BOSTON.

BIM models will never be complete. Models grow over time.

BIG BIM

Phoenix

New York City

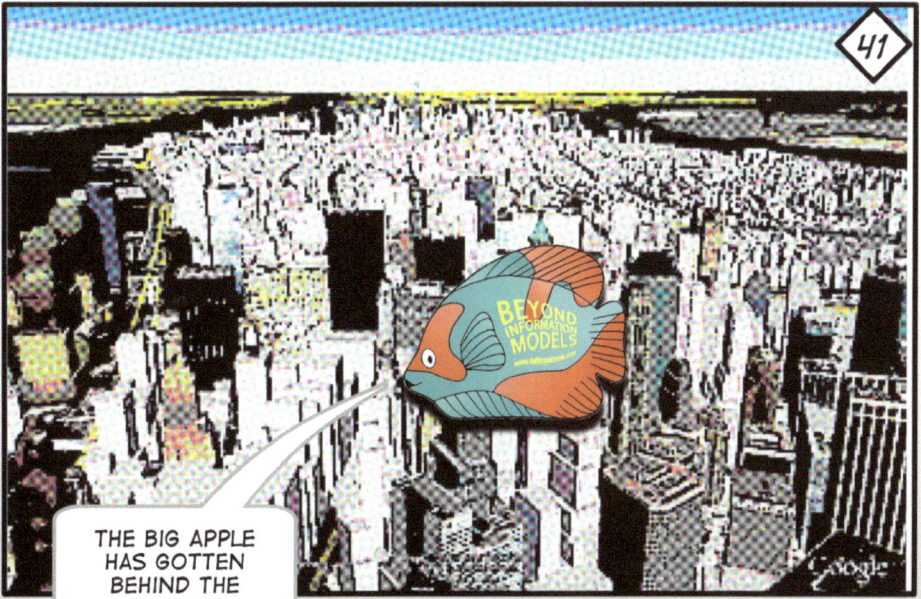

Las Vegas

Oslo

Arizona is a hot-bed of BIM.

People in West Virginia know the benefits of BIM.

Charleston

International buildingSMART Alliance - led from Norway.

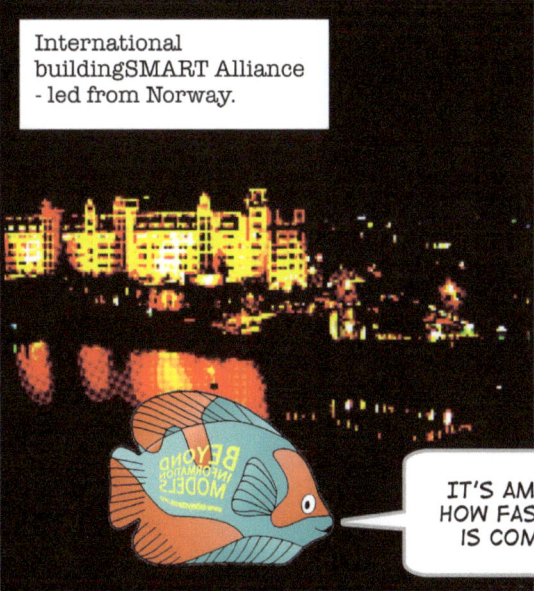

Wisconsin

STATE GOVERNMENTS ARE NOW REQUIRING BIM.

Marina del Rey

BIM is makes recreation efficient.

Salisbury MD

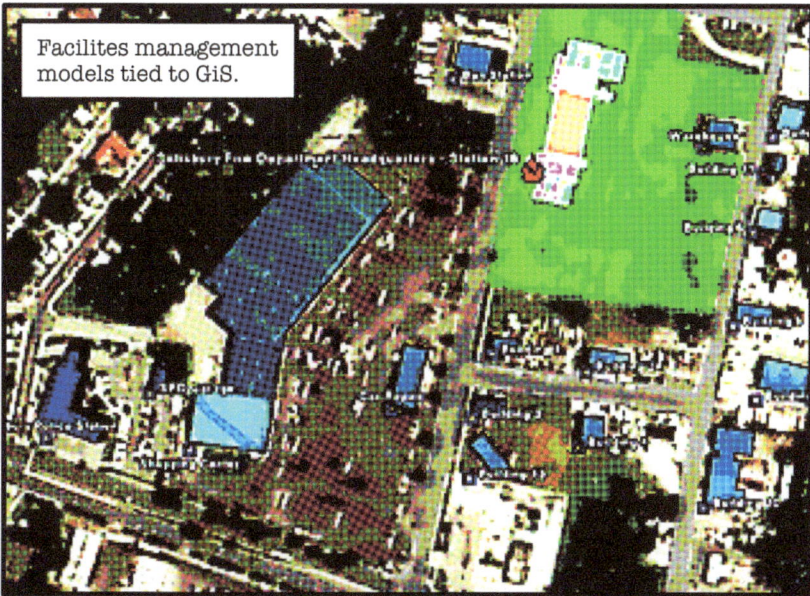
Facilites management models tied to GiS.

- Conflict-free model as project constraint
- bim tools for schedule and $ controls
- Done incorrectly will lose money and time

Control the process in four steps:

1. Identify the constraint
2. Decide how to exploit the constraint
3. Make the constraint important
4. Integrate the constraint into your everyday process

All segments of the business are moving toward BIM

Are you ready?

TODAY

INTEGRATED PROJECTS HAVE REACHED THE TIPPING POINT!

FINITH IS HELPING YOU FIND BIG BIM

BIM and GiS Standards

I remember the blustery winter day in Cleveland where I first saw Keyhole. It seemed like a miracle. For the first time I could visualize geographic data without the baggage that came with GiS. I could zoom into a site and get real-world views, without knowing much about GiS. The limitations revolved around the fact that you had to be part of the Federal government to use Keyhole.

Keyhole then became Google Earth and all was well. Geography and architecture are finally coming together to enable BIG BIM. Yet, buried deep in this wonderful development was a dark secret that could stop development in its tracks. (continued...)

BIM and GiS Standards (continued)

On April 14, 2008 the Open Geospatial Consortium (OGC) adopted KML (Keyhole Markup Language) as an OGC standard, creating the foundation for moving forward with confidence. We can now create and share geographic information directly linked to the design and construction process. We now know that we have a dependable and repeatable way to communicate and amass information, all due to an open standard that makes a very cool product even cooler.

'Who owns the information?' Proprietary information could scuttle the whole system. There needed to be standards...not Google standards; but shared and public standards. Without such standards, Google Earth would continue to be a very cool tool. With such standards it could become the foundation for new ways to do business to achieve real sustainability.

What to do?

- Take off your blinders...
  ### Where are you now?

- Plan strategically...
  ### Where do you want to be?

- Create tactics...
  ### Close the gap!

and...sign up for a BIMstorm at
www.BIMstorm.com

Steps to change

Step 1: Assess readiness
Step 2: Plan strategically
Step 3: Design your future
Step 4: Implement
Step 5: Revisit

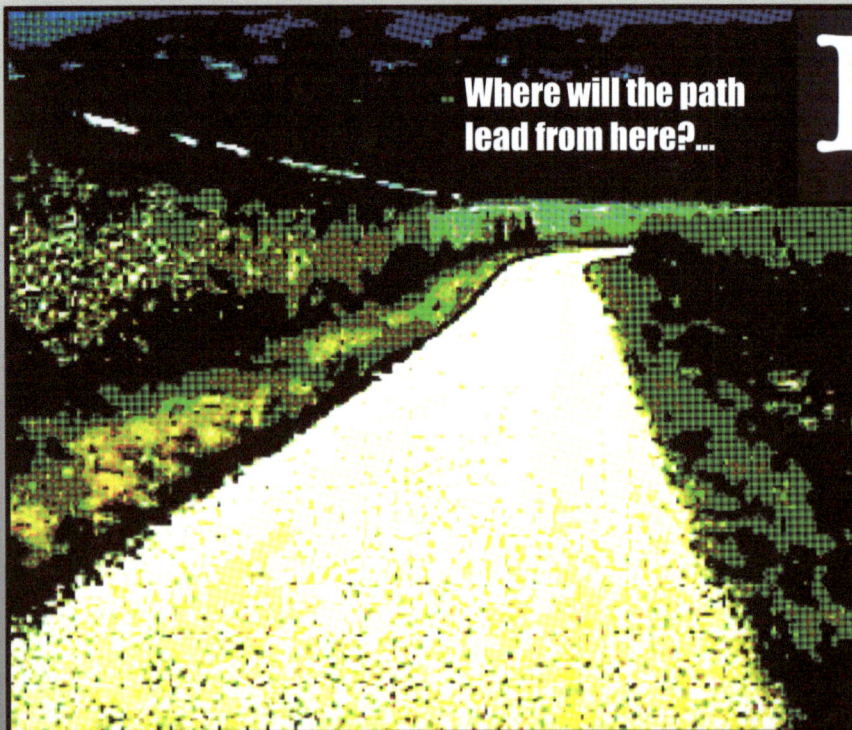

Where will the path lead from here?...

Future

4SITESYSTEMS — BEYOND INFORMATION MODELS

The web started with building the infrastructure for the future. Web 2.0 evolved into platforms for interactivity. Web 3.0 or the Semantic Web, is evolving based on ontologies that define relationships between things. The Future Web will evolve into a full 3D environment where digital environment will simulate reality and extend everywhere.

www.ingramcontent.com/pod-product-compliance
Lightning Source LLC
Chambersburg PA
CBHW061057090426
42742CB00002B/78